Science Museum

Clothes for the job

Catalogue of the collection
in the Science Museum

John E Smart FMA

London Her Majesty's Stationery Office

ISBN 0 11 290429 7

Printed for Her Majesty's Stationery Office by the Roundwood Press
Dd 736278 C20 5/85

Preface

The author wishes to acknowledge the generosity of the specialised and protective wear industry, without which the collection and the catalogue would not have been possible.

I should also like to thank my colleagues, Dr John Griffiths, Mrs Ailsa Jenkins and Dr Anita McConnell for their assistance during the preparation of the text.

John E Smart   1984

Drawings and diagrams prepared in the Science Museum Design Office by Rosemary Pratt.
Photographs, except where marked, by the Science Museum Photographic Studio.

Cover photograph courtesy of the British Steel Corporation.

Contents

Scope of the collection

The Science Museum's collection of specialised and protective wear was begun in 1980 and first exhibited to the public in 1982–3 in a temporary exhibition entitled 'The Great Cover-Up Show', which was sponsored by British Petroleum. A proportion of the collection is displayed on the third floor of the museum and the remaining material is held in the reserve store. Students wishing to see any specimen listed in this catalogue are advised to check beforehand whether it is on display or in reserve before visiting the museum. Reserve material can be seen providing a request is made well in advance.

When this national collection was formed it was known that although existing costume collections in other institutions included material under the heading 'Occupational Dress', this mostly consisted of examples of civil and domestic uniform, simple factory overalls and the like. The more specialised working dress and the ancillary material that went with it had been neglected. The Science Museum collection covers all specialised and protective wear used in industry and some areas of sport. Besides clothing, accessories worn on the person such as filter masks and breathing apparatus, hearing protectors, goggles and so on, are included. Ethnic dress such as Eskimo clothing – although protective – is not included, nor are military or civil uniforms, nor the ordinary overalls such as mechanics or food handlers wear. However, flying clothing, which has become very specialised, and items like police riot helmets, bomb disposal officer's suits and contemporary fabric armour are included. Diving and medical dress are held in other Science Museum collections.

For convenience, this catalogue is divided into sections and the author acknowledges that the appearance of some specimens in one section rather than another, has been a matter of arbitrary personal choice. Each entry includes the museum's inventory number, which should always be quoted in any correspondence, and where a photograph is available the museum negative number is also given. Certain items currently exhibited in the gallery which are on loan from other Science Museum collections are included in this catalogue for the sake of completeness: their entries are starred.

Introduction

It is instinctive to protect one's hands from being burnt when picking up something very hot; we shield our eyes from the glare of a bright light and we wrap up warmly when going out into the cold, so that protective wear is as old as clothing itself. Classical authors such as Homer and Pliny make reference to it: the former to a gardener wearing leather gloves and gaiters to protect him from brambles, the latter to workers using transparent bladder-skin masks to protect themselves from poisonous cinnabar dust.

For many centuries workers improvised protective wear using materials ready to hand. Sometimes, by a process of gradual evolution, this became very effective but often the protection afforded was minimal. It is not until the end of the eighteenth and the beginning of the nineteenth centuries that inventors and designers turned their attention to protective wear. The expansion of industry that took place during the nineteenth century brought many new hazards, but the period also brought a greater awareness of the dangers of industrial disease and accidents. In Britain this led eventually to legislation requiring employers to provide protective clothing and equipment and the consequent growth of an industry to supply them. In this century further legislation, extensive research and the establishment of standards of performance together with the availability of many new materials, have brought a wide variety of clothing and ancillary equipment into use.

Working in areas of extreme cold

In this section specimens rely on either insulation and conservation of body heat or artificial heating to keep the wearer protected. The use of furs as insulating garments goes back to prehistoric times, and the use of padded clothing to early civilizations. Methodical research into problems of keeping warm in cold climates did not really begin until the 1920s and was considerably accelerated during the 1939–45 war.

The Eskimo's clothes get their insulating qualities from natural fur which traps still air in its fibres added to the diving bell principle which retains the heat rising from the body. Synthetic fibre fillings, plastic foams or pile-surfaced cloths serve as insulating barriers in modern clothing. The design of the clothing with close fitting cuffs, double closure over zips, integral hoods, etc., also helps to retain body heat.

Electrically-heated clothing was introduced for air crew in the 1914–18 war. The heating was provided by resistance wires sewn (often in zig-zag fashion for flexibility) to a lightweight garment worn under an insulating outer suit; gloves and boots were heated in the same way. In about 1937 this method was tried for diving suits in America but the brittleness of the wire caused it to be abandoned. Wire of greater flexibility enables modern garments to be produced as knitwear. Within the last year (1983) a metallised fabric which becomes heated when an electric current is passed through it has been produced and made up into garments.

Also included in this section are examples of survival suits. In the early years of the 1939–45 war it was found that many people forced into the sea when an aircraft crashed or a ship sank died not from drowning but from exposure, the cold water chilling their body to the point at which it would not support life. Considerable research was done and now most military air crew wear a survival suit as an integral part of their flying kit while quick-donning suits are provided for ships' crews.

Cold store worker's suit and boots
Nylon quilted over polyester wadding

A two-piece suit intended for men working in the very low temperatures of freezer food stores. The quilted fabric uses polyester wadding to insulate against temperatures as low as −40°C. The zip-fronted jacket has an internal drawstring at the waist to give a close fit. The trousers are elasticated at waist and ankles.

The boots were first marketed in 1981 and have non-slip soles and waterproof uppers. They have a separate inner foam-backed, felt liner which is put on over the wearer's ordinary socks.

Inv. no. 1980–1558   Neg 1093/82/9
Presented by Vacuum Reflex Ltd
Boots
Inv. no. 1981–596
Presented by Plus 50 Protective Footwear Service Ltd

Shackleton Suit (replica) 1924

This style of two-piece suit with integral hood in closely woven gaberdine, based on polar clothing used by Shackleton, was produced for the 1924 Everest expedition. It was worn over thick woollen underwear, a flannel shirt and several sweaters, with several pairs of thick socks or 20ft. elasticated kashmir puttees.

Equipped with this clothing Colonel Norton climbed to 28,000 ft. without oxygen.

Inv. no. 1981–795
Presented by Burberrys Ltd

Helicopter survival suit 1981
Polyurethene coated nylon

The use of helicopters to transfer oil and gas rig workers across the North Sea has created a need for civilian survival suits. This example is issued to staff by the B P Company, to be worn over ordinary working clothes while in transit from shore to rig.

One-way valves release any air trapped in the suit should the helicopter make a forced landing in the sea. In such circumstances the machine often turns completely upside down and survivors must swim out through the submerged doorway. Any air pockets in the survival suit would make this very difficult.

Inv. no. 1982–167
Presented by British Petroleum

Cold store worker's quilted suit and special boots, Inv nos 1980–1558, 1981–596

Civilian helicopter survival suit, inv. no. 1982–167

JOHN FREEMAN

Insulated jacket and trousers
Insulation – metallised spunbonded olefin with 2.5 oz per sq yd polyester fibres

This suit is one of the *Spacecoat* suits made for the Transglobe Expedition and used in the Antarctic and Arctic by Sir Ranulph Fiennes. The suits' insulation lining, SP.27, was developed by NASA for use on space missions and moon landings. It is made from *Tyvek* fabric needle-punched with polyester fibres to produce a pile surfaced cloth. The ventile cloth has been coated to increase washability.

The suit has zips and pockets sealed with a double flap to keep out all wind. Sir Ranulph Fiennes, leader of the expedition, recorded that at the South Pole they experienced wind chill of −70°C (−110°F) – at which temperature exposed flesh freezes in under 25 seconds – but with only a sweater and T-shirt underneath the suits kept them very warm. An earlier version of the garment was produced in 1977 as a housecoat for the elderly to combat hypothermia.

Inv. no. 1983–1057
Lent by Spacecoat Garments Ltd

Heat retention suit 1981
Vinyl backed heavy-duty siliconised rayon over foam lined with aluminium

Designed for use by divers this one-piece coverall would be worn under a 'dry' suit. The fabric's sandwich construction provides for reflection of body heat and insulation, the outer layer is tough and hard wearing. Because the foam is compressed by increasing pressure as the diver goes deeper, the suit's working range is limited.

Inv no. 1983–1067
Presented by Strentex Fabrics Ltd

Cold weather working suit 1982
Multi-ply sandwich of nylon, vinyl, polyester foam, aluminised nylon

A one-piece multi-ply suit intended for workers in sub-zero temperature conditions. A bright aluminised lining assists in the retention of body heat by reflecting it back onto the skin. The seams are sealed to give extra strength and there are inner cuffs and anklets to prevent heat loss.

Manually operated air vents allow the wearer to control the inner temperature to avoid excessive sweating.

Inv. no. 1983–1068
Lent by Strentex Fabrics Ltd

Electrically heated underwear 1980
Knitted terylene yarn with resistance wire incorporated

This set of vest, long pants, socks and gloves was designed for use by aircrew and has electrical resistance wire knitted into the fabric. The outfit operates on 28-volt direct current. The socks and gloves have also been used by armoured fighting vehicle drivers. An example of the glove wired for 6 volt operation (as a demonstration) is also in the collection.

Inv. no. 1980–1555, 1556   Neg 1103/82/11
Presented by Vacuum Reflex Ltd

Electrically heated underwear 1980, Inv no 1980–1555

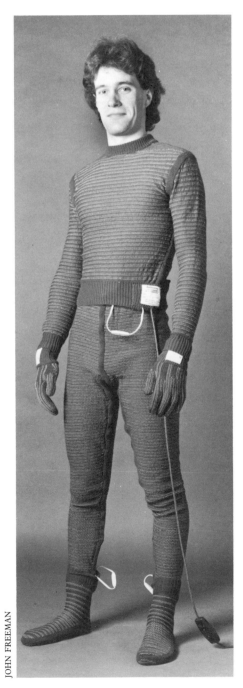

JOHN FREEMAN

Electrically heated waistcoat 1970
Quilted nylon with embedded PVC sheathed resistive elements

A quilted nylon waistcoat incorporating heating elements powered by two nickel cadmium batteries carried inside pockets at the front of the garment. Intended for outdoor workers, it was claimed the waistcoat would give two hours heating for sedentary users and six or eight hours for the more active according to the exertion and natural body heat developed by the user. A free-air type of thermostat controlled the temperature and was pre-set at a mean body skin temperature of 95°F (34°C). The batteries were 18 volt 1.5 amp/hours. Weight with the batteries was 3 lb 2 oz. Manufacture was discontinued because of the problems involved in tailoring the garment incorporating the resistance wires.

Inv. no. 1981–2172
Presented by Stoneleigh Electronics Ltd

Charcoal heater unit and survival bag 1982
Mutli-ply sandwich of nylon, vinyl, polyester foam, aluminised nylon

During nineteenth century winters, ladies carried inside their muffs, small containers holding a block of glowing charcoal. The *Heatapak* unit is a modern development of this idea in which an electrically ignited fuel element generates warm air which is blown through a flexible hose by a small battery powered fan. The fuel element will give warm air for as long as ten hours at about 50°C at the outlet.

The survival bag is made of multi-ply material and has been designed so that the blood pressure and pulse of a casualty can easily be monitored. Individual attention can be given to injured limbs without exposing the whole body and all forms of splint can be accommodated. The bag itself protects against hypothermia and in very low temperatures, or in cases where body heat has already dropped to danger level, the *Heatapak* unit is added.

A special jerkin to which the heater unit can be attached has also been produced.

Inv. no. 1983–1066
Lent by Strentex Fabrics Ltd

Thermal insulation micro-fibres 1978

Thinsulate was first produced in America (US Patent 4118531) by the 3M company in 1978. The insulation derives from micro-fibres which are about ten times finer and so give about twenty times more surface area than the same weight of ordinary synthetic fibres. These new fibres absorb less than 1% of their own weight of water so in damp conditions most of the insulating effect is kept. If down feathers are taken as giving insulation value of 1 an equal thickness of *Thinsulate* has a value of 1.8, ordinary fibres have a value of 0.9 to 1.0. These are small samples only.

Presented by 3M United Kingdom PLC

Thermal insulation fibres 1978

Flectalon was invented by physicists at University College Cardiff (British Patent 1605045) and developed by Porth Textiles Ltd in 1978. The insulation is produced by .0015mm PVC fibres coated with vacuum deposited aluminium only .000020–.000025mm thick. The plastic is non-absorbent and flame-resistant. Compared with down an equal thickness of *Flectalon* has an insulation value of 1.5. The sample fibres are enclosed between transparent plastic for clarity but in normal use, as in the quilted inner socks for rubber boots, the *Flectalon* has an outer fabric casing.

Inv. no. 1982–1768
Presented by Porth Textiles Ltd

Quilted inner socks for rubber boots 1982

This pair of inner socks is insulated with *Flectalon* fibres.

Inv. no. 1982–1769
Presented by Porth Textiles Ltd

Aluminised quilted *Tyvek* suit 1982

The non-woven fabric *Tyvek* has been used to produce this one-piece quilted suit intended for use in warehouses or occasional outside use. The aluminising gives an additional heat retaining quality to the garment.

Inv. no. 1982–742   Neg 261/84
Presented by D H J Industries Ltd

Quilted, aluminised *Tyvek* suit
Inv no 1982–742

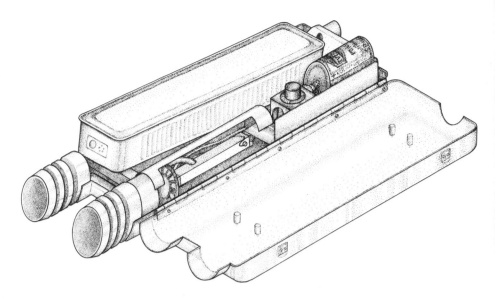

Heatapak unit, Inv. no. 1983–1066.

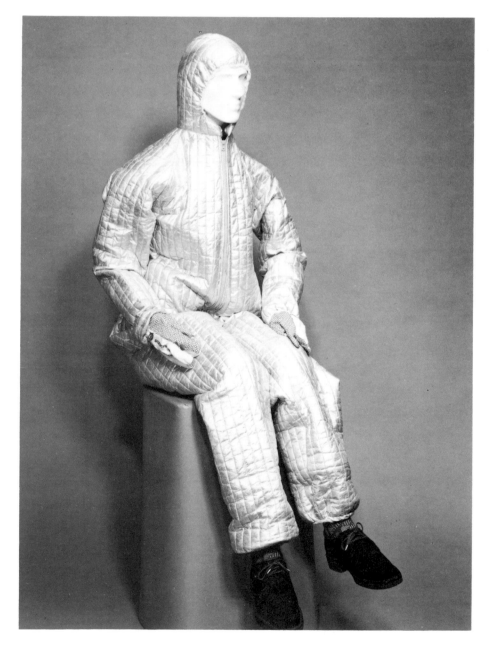

Working in areas of great heat

Specimens in this area divide roughly into two groups: those which provide a shield from heat and those which provide artificial cooling. Insulation of the body from heat has been the traditional method of making it possible to work near furnaces, with workers retiring at intervals to cooler places to recover their normal body temperature. The development of a method of applying a reflective coating of aluminium to fabrics has greatly improved insulation from radiant heat; up to 90% can be reflected away. An additional hazard met in foundries is molten metal splash and a programme of research into the performance of fabrics when splashed with various metals was carried out during the 1970s by the International Wool Secretariat, resulting in the re-classification of fabrics used for foundry clothing.

Artificial cooling can be of two kinds: either simply surrounding the body with a cool atmosphere or carrying the heat away from the body. Research into these methods began in the 1950s, the aim being to keep pilots cool in tropical conditions and during supersonic flight. The RAF Institute of Aviation Medicine at Farnborough produced an undergarment in 1957 which fed cool air onto the wearer's skin. Although this met with some success it was realised that air is not a good heat exchanger and so a garment which carried cool water in a network of flexible pipes was developed in 1962. The British Iron and Steel Trades researchers carried out further work on the air-cooled suit and produced a variation in which the air passing over the body vented into the atmosphere through an air-permeable over-suit giving a marked improvement in the cooling effect.

Around 1974 experiments were carried out in South African mines using an ice cooled jacket when working in conditions of high temperature and humidity. These jackets had pockets of liquid which could be frozen in an ordinary refrigerator and they proved very successful. American scientists developed their own ice jackets for use in mine rescue work and by the beginning of the 1980s, evaluation trials were being made in European coalfields. A British sheet glass manufacturer also introduced such jackets during the late 1970s.

Blast furnace worker's outfit 1981
Wool

These are the clothes formerly worn by Mr Ken Homer, a *Helper* at British Steel Corporation's Redcar Works blast furnace.

The two-piece suit is made from a flame and molten metal splash resistant wool cloth (to BSC Specification MM-1). The safety helmet is glass fibre; this material is preferred in molten metal areas as it resists both heat and metal splash. The face screen is tinted polycarbonate. There are moulder's boots which have quick release fastenings and heat resistant soles. The gloves are made from dust-suppressed asbestos with a chrome leather cuff and are lined with flame resistant thermolate material.

The helmet conforms with BS5240, the face screen to BS2092/m/1, and the boots to BS4676.

Inv. no. 1981–382   Neg 180/84
Presented by the British Steel Corporation

Coke oven worker's outfit 1981
Zirpro treated wool

These are the clothes formerly worn by Mr A Woods a *Coke Oven Operator* at British Steel Corporation's Redcar Works.

The two-piece wool gaberdine suit is lighter in weight than a furnace worker's suit as he does not face such great heat but as the ovens are out of doors the material is water repellent as well as flame resistant. The helmet is ventilated by a small inbuilt fan which circulates clean air down behind the face shield. This special helmet gives respiratory, head, eye and face protection. His feet were protected by standard safety boots. The gloves are chrome leather/cotton.

Inv. no. 1981–383   Neg 213/84
Presented by British Steel Corporation
Safety boots shown with this outfit
presented by Itex Safety Ltd
Inv. No. 1983–1276.

German Furnaceman's Jacket and Trousers 1982
Cotton treated with a derivative of THPS (tetrakis hydroxymethyl phosphonium sulphate)

Intended for use in iron and steel works the suit is made from heavyweight cotton 'moleskin' cloth treated with *Proban*. Certain German manufacturers prefer to use this cloth – which withstands molten metal splash – because of the ease of laundering.

Inv. no. 1982–1797
Presented by Albright & Wilson Ltd

Furnace worker's smock 1980

Heat can be reflected just like light and coating a fabric with a bright reflecting surface greatly improves its heat shielding qualities. This *Gentex* smock of aluminised rayon effectively screens radiant heat but gives only limited protection against metal-spatter.

Inv. no. 1980–1591
Presented by Jelaco Ltd

Blast furnace worker's outfit 1981,
Inv no 1981–382

Foundryman's jacket and trousers 1981

A jacket and trousers in heavyweight wool fabric, anti-metal splash and fire resistant to BS3119 and 3120.

Inv. no. 1981–456
Presented by Greenham Tool Co

Coke oven worker's outfit 1981,
Inv no 1981–383

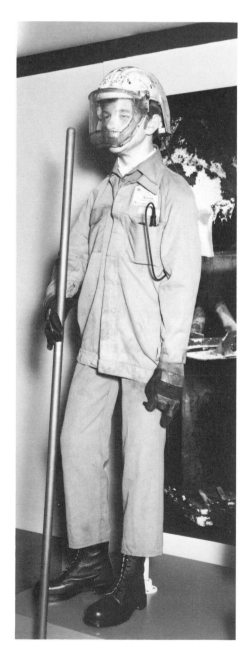

Furnaceman's ice jacket 1981
Cotton drill, ceramic fibre insulated shoulders

The jacket has pockets holding ten standard, picnic basket icepacks and is worn under a woollen or metallised jacket and over the vest or sweat shirt.

Inv. no. 1981–1501
Presented by Pilkington Brothers PLC

Glass furnaceman's clothing 1981
Natural wool, cotton underwear

Flat glass making requires the continuous operation of furnaces and the men attending the furnace are exposed to great heat. The normal wear is this two-piece woollen 'gladding' suit, over a mesh singlet and long johns. The mesh underwear not only insulates but lessens skin pain as there is only point contact with the hot layers of fabric. The large brimmed hat shields the eyes when pulled well down. An alternative hat with side curtains is also in the collection and in extreme heat a mesh *Nomex* veil would be pinned in front of the face. Another dome-shaped hat is also preserved with these items.

Inv. No. 1981–1500, 1503, 1504
Presented by Pilkington Brothers PLC

Foundry worker's smock and hood 1980
Wool, and aluminised coated wool

A smock and hood designed to be worn over a man's ordinary working clothes in situations where over-all protection is not necessary. The *Multitect* smock is a wool fabric giving metal splash protection up to 1650°C and is flame resistant to BS3120. The lighter weight fabric of the hood has been metallised to give better heat protection.

Inv. no. 1980–1560
Presented by Multifabs Ltd

Insulated jacket and hood 1981

A jacket and hood in *Nomex* fabric insulated with ceramic fibre padding and worn under a standard furnaceman's woollen or metallised fabric suit to give additional insulation from heat.

Inv. no. 1981–1502
Presented by Pilkington Brothers PLC

Air ventilated engine room suit
Neoprene coated terylene, helmet in methyl methylcrylate

Before entering a nuclear fall-out zone Naval ships would need to close down all external ventilation to exclude radio-active particles. In exercises the engine spaces became too hot for crewmen to work in and this type of suit was designed to overcome the problem. Installation of remote controls has now made the suit obsolescent.

The suit is in two layers; an inner sandwich of plastic film separated by loosely woven plastic and ventilated by pumped air, over this is worn the outer, insulated, coated terylene garment lined with quilted plastic. The inner garment is perforated to allow the air to come into contact with the skin. Air is fed into the suit via a Hilsch vortex tube supported in a harness worn over the outer garment.

Inv. no. 1983–1076   Neg 1094/82/6
Lent by Ministry of Defence (Navy)

Glass furnaceman's clothing, Inv. no. 1981–1500.

Ice-cooled jacket used in South African mines c. 1974

In very deep mines it is so hot that men cannot work efficiently. Between 1971 and 1974 this problem was investigated in South African gold mines. Colder air could not be circulated round the mine galleries, so this ice-cooled jacket was designed as an alternative.

The inner poncho-type vest has 26 water-filled sealed pockets (weighing 4.5 kg) which are frozen in a special refrigerator. The ice, insulated from the hot atmosphere by the outer jacket, keeps the miner cool for about 2½ hours.

Inv. no. 1984–186   Neg 909/83
Lent by G W Crockford

South African miner's ice jacket c1974,
Inv no 1984–186

Air ventilated engine room suit,
Inv no 1983–1076

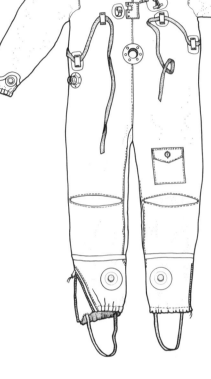

JOHN FREEMAN

8

Fire resistant clothing

Pliny in his 'Natural History' records the use of asbestos fabric as 'royal funeral shrouds' – to keep the ashes separate from those of the funeral pyre – and as dinner napkins – which could be cleaned by throwing them in the fire. Until large deposits of asbestos were discovered in Canada during the nineteenth century, the fabric was too costly for general use in industry. Following this discovery, large factories with machinery for spinning and weaving asbestos fibres were established and turned out quantities of fire resistant fabrics. Asbestos is also an effective insulator and so there were many applications for the fabric both to resist fire and heat. The first asbestos suits for entering, or working in close proximity to, flames were introduced in about 1936. Aluminising asbestos to reflect away some of the heat was first tried in the 1920s, but the process of applying it was unsatisfactory and a successful method of applying the aluminium was only developed in the 1950s. Although the fabric can be coated to avoid any dusting of the asbestos, fears of possible health risks are leading to its abandonment but it still remains the standard by which other fabrics are judged. Man-made fibres now form the basis of clothing fabrics likely to receive long exposure to fire and flames and the collection includes examples of most of these.

Fabrics were initially given protection from short term exposure to flame by dipping them in a solution of borax (ammonium chlorate); unfortunately washing will remove the treatment as will prolonged exposure to vibration. Modern chemical treatments alter the nature of the textile, in some cases forming a polymer within the fibres, without changing handling characteristics.

Aluminised asbestos fire suit 1981

Aluminised asbestos suit and gauntlet gloves
Glass fibre polyester resin helmet with aluminium pigment surface and aluminised asbestos neck curtain
Helmet visor in polycarbonate sandwiching wiregauze
Chrome leather hide boots, waterproofed with neoprene outer sole

A one-piece suit worn over string and woollen undergarments and intended for close proximity fire fighting out of doors. It gives sufficient protection against heat and flame to allow snatch rescues from burning aircraft (where temperatures can reach 1000°C) or to enable externally placed valves to be shut off in fires at petro-chemical works.

Despite its stiff appearance the suit is light and flexible and can be donned by experienced personnel in about 12 seconds.

Raglan sleeves prevent the wrists becoming exposed when the wearer raises his arms. The gauntlets have elasticated wrists to prevent them from slipping off.

Inv. no. 1981–396   Neg 1428/82
Lent by Bristol Uniforms Ltd

Close proximity aluminised rayon fire suit 1981

Aluminised rayon suit and gauntlet gloves
Heavy duty glassfibre helmet with aluminised glass wool neck curtain and polycarbonate visor
Chrome hide leather boots with nitrile rubber sole and steel toe cap

The *Bristol Marine* suit was designed for close proximity fire fighting. Since the suit is in two pieces it would not be worn where there was a likelihood of flames 'licking' the wearer. A one-piece garment gives more protection from flame 'lick'. This two-piece garment, however, has the advantage that the jacket can be removed between active operations.

Inv. no. 1981–397   Neg as above
Lent by Bristol Uniforms Ltd

Shipboard fire fighting suit 1981

Modacrylic beta-glass fibre yarn mixture cloth (lined with non-flammable twill) coat, trousers and gauntlet mittens
Heavy duty glassfibre helmet with Heatshield cloth neck curtain and polycarbonate visor
Chrome hide leather boots with nitrile rubber sole and steel toe cap

The *Bristol Fleet* suit was designed primarily for use on board ship following the SOLAS (Safety of Life at Sea) regulations of 1974 which required vessels to carry specialised safety equipment, including protective clothing.

This two piece suit is made of lined *Heatshield* cloth which will maintain its structure in flames of up to 1000°C. It protects from intense radiant heat, though not from flames, and also gives limited protection against cold, most acids, oils and other chemicals.

The wrists and ankles are elasticated to avoid exposing areas to radiant heat.

Inv. no. 1981–398   Neg as above
Lent by Bristol Uniforms Ltd

Anti-flash gas welder's suit

Modacrylic beta-glass fibre yarn mixture cloth overall and gauntlet mittens
Anti-flash hood with polycarbonate visor and integral heavy duty helmet
Chrome hide leather boots with nitrile rubber sole and steel toe cap

An outfit designed for British Gas Council workmen inspecting high pressure natural gas pipes. Made of unlined *Heatshield* cloth the suit will give up to 20 seconds protection against flames at 850°C before the heat penetrates to the skin and becomes painful. Since *Heatshield* is light and flexible the garment is similar to an ordinary working overall. The hood is designed to fit round breathing apparatus and over an industrial helmet. It is fitted with a wide vision polycarbonate visor.

Inv. no. 1981–399
Lent by Bristol Uniforms Ltd

Sections of fire fighting suits

1 *Aluminised wool felt* suitable for a very lightweight fire proximity suit.
2 *Aluminised asbestos lined with wool felt* suitable for far longer duration close proximity to fires than material No. 1. It can also be used for very short duration fire entry if made up into a one-piece suit.
3 *Double layer of aluminised asbestos with asbestos insulation* suitable for a rather heavy and bulky fire entry suit.

Inv. no. 1982–411
Presented by Bestobell Engineering Products Ltd

Fire fighting suits,
Inv nos 1981–396, 398, 397

Protective suit in carbon fibre material
1981

Mr David Cox, an employee of Payne's Fireworks Ltd., wore this suit to light the large catherine wheel in the Royal Wedding display in July 1981. The suit's outer fabric is of flame resistant *Panotex* carbon fibre introduced that same year. The insulating layer (beneath the outer fabric) is of *Panotex* felt the short fibres of which help to reduce conduction of heat through to the body. An inner charcoal cloth lining absorbs perspiration.

The suit was coloured black so that Mr Cox was invisible to the watching public and television cameras.

Panotex is woven carbon fibres (with 8.5% wool) coated with silicon resin.

Inv. no. 1983–865
Lent by Universal Carbon Fibres Ltd

Fire resistant overalls
Aromatic nylonid polyamide

These overalls are designed for welders and others working in fire-risk areas. The suit's material is *Nomex III*, first produced in 1961 by Du Pont, which has the special property that when it is subjected to a flame the pores in the fabric close up and the fabric's thickness increases.

Inv. no. 1980–1601
Presented by Nicholson's (Overalls) Ltd

Boiler suit in fireproof cotton
Cotton treated with a derivative of THPS (tetrakis hydroxymethyl phosphonium sulphate)

This overall is made from cotton treated by the *Proban* process. The resultant fabric is virtually indistinguishable from the original cotton except that it is flame retardant and about 15–20% heavier. The natural comfort of the cotton fabric is unaffected by the treatment, which forms an insoluble polymer inside the fibre which remains there for the life-time of the garment.

When flames come into contact with *Proban* cotton it forms a strong solid char which immediately insulates the wearer against the heat of the flame.

Overalls made from this material are worn during flight by the NASA astronauts aboard the Space Shuttle Orbiter.

Inv. no. 1982–1798
Presented by Albright and Wilson Ltd

Foul weather clothing

The need to keep dry in bad weather to avoid loss of efficiency, ill-health, or even death from exposure is now well understood. One of the problems has always been that a garment which keeps all water out also keeps in the water vapour produced by our bodies: such fabrics are called non-ventile. In humid conditions the inside of such a garment can become unpleasantly damp and provides a route by which body heat can rapidly escape. Not until the late 1970s were efficient ventile waterproof fabrics produced which permitted the water vapour to pass through.

The earliest waterproof materials were oilskin and tarpaulin, produced by coating ordinary cloth with linseed oil in one case and tar in the other. Rubberised cloth was introduced in the early nineteenth century, Mackintosh patenting the method of spreading natural rubber to make a thin sheet while Goodyear and others patented methods of vulcanising the rubber to make it stable and of making cloth water-repellent by chemical treatment. Until the 1950s these were the only materials for making foul weather clothing. The introduction of PVC either as an unsupported sheet or as a coating on a woven cloth was an important development, although early PVC sheet became hard and less flexible in cold weather and could tear easily when unsupported. Following PVC came another plastic, Polyurethane, now widely used as a coating for proofed fabrics.

Improvements continued in chemical treatments to ventile fabrics yet the problem still remained that under certain circumstances they let in water. The development of microcellular plastic sheet in the late 1970s produced a material which would allow water vapour to pass through the microscopic holes in the material but the same holes were too small to pass liquid. Applied to a fabric it could be made up into garments that were both waterproof and ventile.

Rain suit in supported PVC
Sandwich of polyvinylchloride, nylon fabric, polyvinylchloride

The simplest and cheapest form of waterproof clothing is that made from thin sheet plastic such as PVC. In the 1950s when these garments were introduced it was found that in industrial situations the plastic film tore easily. By applying the plastic film to a woven cloth greater resistance to tearing was obtained.

The fabric of this *Rainmaster* suit is a PVC, textile, PVC sandwich and the seams are both stitched and welded. A high visibility orange dye has been incorporated into the plastic to enable the wearer to be seen more easily in the poor light of rainy days.

Inv. no. 1980–1587
Presented by Safety Specialists Ltd

Crossing-patrol coat and hat
Polyurethane-coated stretch nylon

This light-weight coat and hat are made of a completely waterproof fabric. Because they are worn only briefly the problem of retention of water vapour from the wearer's body can be disregarded. In warm weather the coat can be left open for ventilation.

This garment is white for easy identification by motorists and is made more conspicuous by adding *Scotchlite* reflective panels.

Inv. no. 1980–1797
Presented by Bristol Oilskin & Overall Co Ltd

Weatherproof jacket and trousers in a ventile fabric
Sandwich of nylon fabric, polyurethane foam, polyurethane film, polyurethane foam, nylon fabric

A two-piece outfit intended for executive wear and made from *Brollibond* fabric. This ventile fabric is waterproofed by a thin plastic film incorporated in the five layers which forms a bonded ply. Water vapour from the wearer's body is released as it migrates through the inner foam layer and evaporates from the edges of the garments. The fabric is also flame-retardant and crease-resistant.

Inv. no. 1980–1798
Presented by Bristol Oilskin & Overall Co Ltd

Foul weather jacket with impervious seams

Seams are the weakest part of rainwear clothing for water can penetrate ordinary machine stitched joins in fabric. The Jeltek Company devised and patented the *Unistrate* seam in February 1973. The seam is produced by inserting a strip of thermoplastic between the fabric edges and then, after the seam has been stitched twice, passing it over a high frequency heater to seal the seam.

This jacket, which has *Unistrate* seams, is an updated version of a design which received an award from the Minister of Public Building & Works in 1968 for an outdoor working suit. The fabric is a lightweight coated nylon and the complete jacket weights only 850 grams (28 oz).

This fabric is non-ventile so the jacket is ventilated by attaching the shoulder yoke to give downward-opening vents. As the wearer moves his body and arms these vents automatically release the moisture-laden air. The yoke also avoids any upward-facing seams on the shoulders.

Inv. no. 1981–713   Neg 1673/82
Presented by Jeltek Ltd

Antistatic weatherproof two-piece suit
Modified polyvinylchloride-coated nylon

Police and rescue teams attending accidents where petrol has been spilt are at risk from the inflammable gases which a small spark could easily ignite. Many coated fabrics will build up a static electric charge on their surface as layers of clothing rub against each other. If this electricity discharges to earth a spark may be produced. To prevent this build up, a plastic fabric may be made conductive by adding a 'spray-on' layer of chemical or, as in this case, incorporating an extra ingredient in the PVC coating mix. It is preferable to add the antistatic chemical to the coating mixture as an outer layer may in a short time be lost through wear.

Inv. no. 1981–714   Neg as above
Presented by Jeltek Ltd

Royal Marine raiding craft Coxswain's immersion suit
Nylon/butyl/nylon laminated fabric

The suit is fully waterproof with natural latex neck and wrist seals cut in one piece with a long diagonal water-tight zip allowing front entry. The suit has been designed with very roomy underarm sections to allow the wearer to stretch his arms above his head without straining or bursting the seams.

Across the back waistline there is an extra gusset of material making it easier to get into the upper part of the suit. After donning the suit the wearer closes off the gusset by means of a zip.

The external pockets have drain holes. The gloves, waterproof socks, boots and hood are all separate items.

Inv. no. 1983–1077
Lent by the Ministry of Defence (Royal Navy)

Royal Navy foul weather suit 1950s to 1970s
PVC coated nylon

Naval crewmen continued to use the traditional oilskins until they were replaced by these black PVC-coated suits. The smock top has an integral hood.

Inv. no. 1982–1771
Presented by the Ministry of Defence (Royal Navy)

Jacket with impervious seams (*Weatherguard*) inv. no. 1981–713

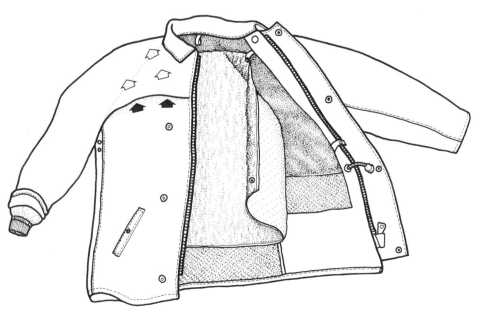

Royal Navy foul weather suit 1982
Polyurethane-coated nylon

The black PVC coated suits were replaced in the 1980s by this new design which is a zip fronted anorak and trousers; the anorak's hood replaces the traditional sou' wester.

The material is a heavyweight coated nylon cloth with a lightweight lining of the same material. The inner lining can be drawn tight at the wrists using *Velcro* strips and the trouser bottoms can be closed to the sea boots in the same way. The hood has a stiffened peak and a padded frame around the face opening; there are straps over the crown to adjust the hood to fit more closely when a seaman is wearing headphones. A *Velcro* fastened weather strip over the zip gives added protection against wind-driven rain and spray.

Inv. no. 1983–1156
Lent by Compton Webb Group Marketing Ltd

Fishery protection crewman's suit 1982
Polyurethane coated nylon

Royal Navy crewmen on Fishery Protection duties regularly need to go by small inflatable boat from their own ship to fishing vessels, often in bad weather conditions. When inspecting a fishing vessel the men must visit very confined spaces and face the hazards of moving about on decks cluttered with fishing gear. Their suits must not only keep them dry during the boat journey but also have to be resistant to snagging and tearing and reasonably comfortable to wear when moving about the fishing vessel. This example is a one-piece coverall in coated nylon developed from the civilian helicopter survival suit. Should the boat overturn during the passage between vessels the suit also gives survival protection. An arduous duty lifejacket is worn with the suit.

Inv. no. 1983–1354
Lent by Multifabs Ltd

Royal Marine coxswain's immersion suit, inv. no. 1983–1077

Sample pieces of waterproof, windproof and ventile fabric and PTFE film
Polytetrafluoroethylene microporous film bonded to textiles

Gore-tex† fabrics are a family of materials combining ventile fabrics and a microporous polymeric film. This film of expanded PTFE has 9 billion pores per square inch. Each pore is 20,000 times smaller than a drop of water yet 700 times larger than a molecule of water vapour. Liquid cannot penetrate the film but water vapour from the body can escape. The large volume of small pores also reduces the air permeability of the fabric giving protection from chilling winds. The microporous film is combined with standard fabrics such as nylon, polyester and polyester cotton to produce a really effective ventile yet waterproof fabric. Besides their use in foul weather clothing the fabrics are also valuable in the medical and industrial sectors for their acid splash protection, flame retardancy, and as bacteriological barriers.

†*Gore-tex* is a trademark used by W L Gore & Associates Incorporated.
Presented by W L Gore & Associates (UK) Ltd.

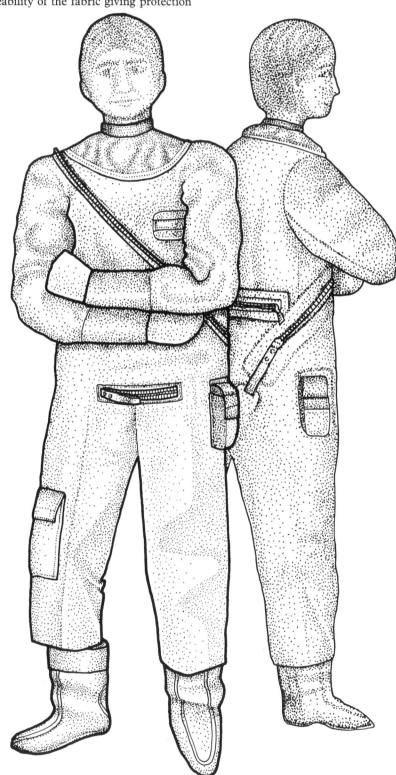

Flying clothing

The first flyers faced two hazards: cold and lack of oxygen. Balloonists and early pilots relied on ordinary winter wear to keep them warm. At first only balloonists went high enough to need oxygen, the operational ceiling of aircraft remained fairly low until the coming of the first world war and then rather primitive oxygen apparatus was devised for the aircrew. As already noted electrically-heated clothing was also introduced during that same period.

The development of civil aviation brought closed cockpits and pressurised cabins making it possible for crew members to wear ordinary uniform clothing; however, military pilots continued to need protection against cold and lack of oxygen.

In the 1930s attempts on altitude records led to the development of very specialised flying clothing including pressurised flying suits, for at great heights the lack of air pressure on the body must be replaced artificially. After the 1939–45 war the increasing performance of military aircraft, extending the height and speed at which they operated, brought further elaboration in air crew clothing. Finally, for manned space flights, we have seen the development of the space suit, enclosing the wearer in a complete life-supporting environment when he meets the zero gravity, high-vacuum conditions beyond our atmosphere.

Aeroplane outfit c. 1910 (replica)
Gaberdine lined with camel fleece
Leather gauntlets

The original outfit was manufactured by Burberrys Ltd, during the early years of flying, comprising tunic, breeches and boots worn with puttees, together with a fabric helmet.

The material is gaberdine lined with camel fleece. It kept the aviator warm without restricting his movement.

Inv. no. 1982–422
Fabric supplied by Burberrys Ltd

World War 1 Sidcot Suit*

The Sidcot suit, named after its inventor Sidney Cotton, was popular during the latter part of WW1 and for many years after. Three fabrics made up the suit: fur inside, silk interlining, and gaberdine cover. The pilot is kept warm by his own body heat trapped inside the closely-woven silk.

Goggles of splinterproof *Triplex* glass and a leather mask protected the pilot's face. To complete the outfit the pilot wore furlined leather gauntlets and knee-length leather boots.

Inv. No. 1981–2035   Neg 1273/81
Purchased

1910 'Outrig' style flying suit, inv. no. 1982–422

World War II Bomber Crew Flying Clothing

To overcome the severe cold, bomber crews often wore fleece-lined leather flying jacket and trousers over a uniform. They provided insulation but tended to be rather bulky for the confined spaces of a bomber. The suits ceased to be issued in 1949 but many are still in use today by pilots of vintage aircraft.

The helmet is RAF type B (introduced in 1935); this example is modified to take Gosport tubes. Mk VIII goggles (1943) were worn until the 1960s by certain aircrew. The oxygen mask, type K, is complete with microphone, lead and mask tube. Cape leather flying gauntlets and 1941 pattern knee length boots complete the outfit.

Inv. no. 1984–247
Lent by the Royal Air Force Museum, Hendon

Full pressure suit type B *c.* 1960★
Terylene sail cloth (white) lined with nylon (butyl-nylon)
Melinex (mylar) hood lined with clear terylene

This suit was developed at the Royal Aircraft Establishment, Farnborough. When inflated to 2.5 psi air flows over the body and out through an opening in the neck. The suit is light to wear and easy to put on, with a full-length zipper from crotch up to neck.

When the suit is pressurised the wearer loses much of his mobility, but three-axis (all round) arm movement is possible by means of a 'gimbal cord' arrangement at the shoulders. If pressure drops in the cabin an automatic air supply closes the helmet within one-twentieth second.

This helmet design has been nicknamed the 'handbag'.

Inv. no. 1980–452
Presented by the Royal Aircraft Establishment, Farnborough   Neg 214/84

The collection also has another type B suit (lent by the Royal Aircraft Establishment) in green material. This example is of the same design as Inv. no. 1980–452 but is a later model.

Inv. no. 1983–686.

Pilot's type B full pressure suit c1960, Inv no 1980–452

Aircrew equipment for high altitude flying

A Phantom jet pilot flying at over 16,500m wears a three-layered outfit. Over cotton underwear a combined partial pressure anti-'g' air-ventilated suit (Mk 2) is worn. This provides protection against loss of cabin pressure and large 'g' forces as well as keeping the pilot cool by blowing air over the skin. The final outer immersion coverall (Mk 10) can provide over 12 hours protection in water over 50°C (41°F)

To complete the outfit the following items can be worn:
Boots, 1965 pattern
Water resistant (Cape leather) gloves
Life preserver, MK 10, complete with torso harness
Helmet, Mk 3C
Oxygen regulator, type 324
Oxygen mask, type P.
Examples are preserved with the outfit.

Inv. no. 1984–190
Lent by the Institute of Aviation Medicine, Farnborough

William Anders' Apollo 8 space suit 1968, Inv no 1973–399

World War I Sidcot suit, Inv. no. 1981–2035

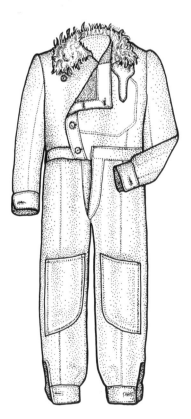

16

Apollo 8 space suit 1968★

This suit was originally worn by William Anders on the Apollo 8 mission of Christmas 1968 in the first flight around the moon. Intended to give full protection against the harsh conditions of space the fabric of the suit is multilayered (see Inv no 1976–590 below) the outer material being *Teflon* coated beta cloth.

Inv. no. 1973–399
Lent by the National Air and Space Museum, Washington D.C.   Neg 851/82

Section of Apollo Space Suit★

Against the skin, the Apollo EVA (Extra Vehicular Activity) suit has a liquid-cooled undergarment (similar to Inv. no. 1983–687 pt below). Next comes a layer of lightweight heat-resistant *Nomex* (1) followed by a gas-tight bladder of neoprene-coated nylon (2) and a nylon restraint layer (3) to prevent the bladder from ballooning outwards. Thermal and micrometeroid protection is provided by a neoprene-coated nylon ripstop layer (4), alternating layers of perforated aluminised *Mylar* film (5, 7, 9, 11 and 13) and non-woven *Dacron* (6, 8, 10 and 12), two layers of super *Kapton* (14 and 15) and finally outer layers of beta cloth (16) and *Teflon* fabric (17).

Inv. no. 1976–590
Lent by the National Air and Space Museum, Washington D.C.

Section of Shuttle Space Suit★

Unlike the space suits used in the Apollo or Skylab programs, where the entire space suit was custom manufactured for a specific astronaut, the Shuttle space suit is comprised of separate components which can be assembled to fit almost anyone (male or female).

A typical cross-section of the suit is 11 layers deep consisting of the Liquid Cooling Ventilation Garment (LCVG) (2 layers); the pressure retention garment (2 layers); and the Thermal Micrometeoroid Garment (TMG) (7 layers). The LCVG maintains astronaut comfort, the pressure retention garment provides containment of the breathing air and the TMG protects against micrometeoroids and insulates against the extreme temperatures of space.

Inv. no. 1984–322
Presented by ILC Dover, Delaware

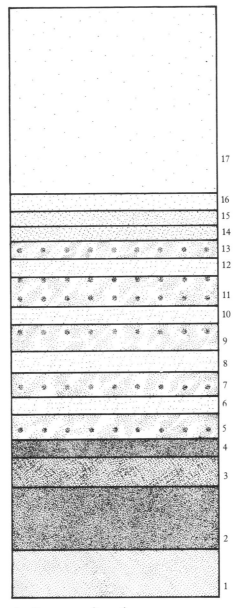

Apollo space suit section,
Inv. no. 1976–590

Air ventilated suit c. 1957

Air ventilated suits are worn in many high performance aircraft, mainly in tropical areas. They are worn under pressure or immersion suits and are in the form of a mesh coverall supporting a network of tubes.

Air is forced into the tubes and out through small holes just above the skin, keeping the pilot cool and dry. The air supply is obtained from trapped engine air, cooled by a heat exchanger. One serious disadvantage of this system is that contaminated air must be filtered. These filters are bulky, difficult to install in modern military aircraft and they tend to reheat the cooled air supply.

Inv. no. 1983–687 pt.
Lent by the Royal Aircraft Establishment, Farnborough

Water-cooled suit c. 1965

This liquid conditioned suit consists of an undergarment with a network of small pipes (approximately 150 metres in total) enclosed in fabric tunnels, attached to the inner surface. Water, plus ethylene glycol (antifreeze) enters through ducts in the wrists and ankles, flows centrally to the trunk and collects in a series of outlet manifolds before returning to the supply system.

The flowing liquid absorbs body heat and loses it through a heat exchanger before recirculating through the suit.

Inv. no. 1983–687 pt.
Lent by the Royal Aircraft Establishment, Farnborough

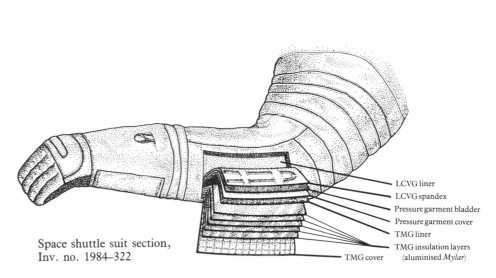

Space shuttle suit section,
Inv. no. 1984–322

LCVG liner
LCVG spandex
Pressure garment bladder
Pressure garment cover
TMG liner
TMG insulation layers (aluminised *Mylar*)
TMG cover

Flying Helmet *c.* 1914*

During the early years of flight aeroplanes were notorious for their bumpy landings. Many pilots, therefore, chose to wear helmets like this example (made by *Tautz & Co*) to protect their heads in case of accident. The curious acorn shape made from some unidentified composition is approximately 10 mm thick and covered in leather.

Inv. no. 1936–402   Neg. 250/84
Lent by the Ministry of Defence (Air)

Dutch flying helmet *c.* 1930

This was used by W Kuyper, of the Netherlands Air Force. The design is identical to those made by Roold of Paris which first appeared in 1912. The helmet is made from thick cork covered in painted fabric with chin strap and heavily padded ear flaps in leather. The shape is similar to Inv. no. 1936–402.

Inv. no. 1984–242
Lent by Aviodome, Schipol

Type C flying helmet *c.* 1946*

A type first issued to the RAF in 1941. The exterior is in tough chrome leather, the inner lining in soft chamois. This example has an oxygen mask and microphone attached.

Inv. no. 1977–567
Purchased

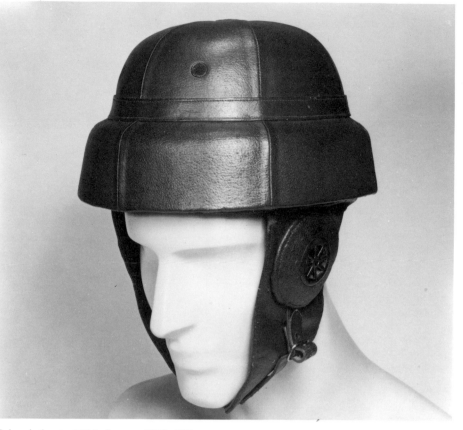

Flying helmet c1914, Inv no 1936–402

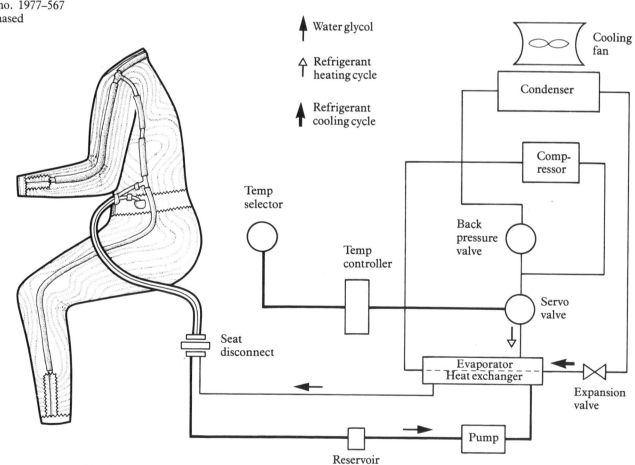

Liquid cooled suit circuit, see
Inv. no. 1983–687

18

Partial pressure flying helmet, type A, 1952

This helmet, together with Inv. nos. 1983–689 and 1983–690 were developed and tested at the Royal Aircraft Establishment, Farnborough, England. Type A was worn with a United States capstan partial pressure suit.

Inv. no. 1983–688   Neg 929/83
Lent by the Royal Aircraft Establishment Museum

Partial pressure flying helmet, c. 1955

Designed as an anti-blast helmet, this helmet is fitted with an automatic barometric device which senses a sudden cabin decompression and closes the visor. To prevent misting the visor is of double-layered construction.

Inv. no. 1983–689   Neg 928/83
Lent by Royal Aircraft Establishment Museum

Partial pressure flying helmet c. 1958

This was the final model of the 1955 helmet (1983–689). The oxygen supply valves are plastic and the visor is electrically heated.

Inv. no. 1983–690   Neg 926/83
Lent by Royal Aircraft Establishment Museum

Partial pressure flying helmet type A c1952,
Inv no 1983–688

Partial pressure flying helmet c1955,
Inv no 1983–689

Partial pressure flying helmet c1958,
Inv no 1983–690

19

Chemical handling and gas-tight clothing

There are occasions – if chemicals are spilled or contaminated areas must be cleaned or inspected – when people must come into contact with substances or gases that are hazardous to life. In the last century the only available protection was a modified rubberised canvas diving suit worn with either tube-to-helmet apparatus or a self-contained breathing set. There are now many kinds of suits, made in one or two pieces; the simplest merely keep off acid splashes whilst the more complex ones are completely gas-tight and afford safety in the most hazardous situations. The introduction of synthetic rubber and various plastics has meant that a choice of materials is available to the designer to provide protection against chemicals and gases. In addition to suits worn with filter masks or breathing apparatus modern variations on the old tube-to-helmet apparatus now feed the air supply into the whole suit so that it partially inflates, both ventilating and cooling it.

The wearing of a fully gas-tight suit places great mental and physical strain on the person using it. Firemen who have to wear such suits to deal with spillages can usually only work hard for about 20 minutes before needing to be relieved because of the onset of heat exhaustion.

Air ventilated full suit
Polyvinylchloride sheet

Suits like this are often used in industries where it is important to protect a worker from toxic dusts and vapours. Air, fed into the suit via the airline, exhausts through one-way valves inside short sleeves which hang from the suit. The seams of the suit are high-frequency welded and the zip is gas-tight.

Inv. no. 1980–1416
Presented by Plysu Industrial Ltd

Chemical hazard suit
Polyvinyl chloride (PVC) coated nylon

The design of this one-piece suit conforms to Home Office specifications. There is a double thickness of material on the back so that a breathing set can be worn without damaging the suit. The front of the suit is fastened by a heavy duty zipper covered by a double flap which is attached by *Velcro*.

Inv. no. 1980–1561   Neg 212/84
Presented by Multifabs Ltd

Chemical hazard suit 1980,
Inv no 1980–1561

Chemical resistant cap, jacket and trousers
PVC proofed, low-twist nylon fabric.
Visor in high density polyethylene

This *Northylon* outfit gives full-cover protection against acids, alkalis, solvents and other noxious substances. The suit is polyvinyl chloride (PVC) coated nylon, a combination which resists most chemicals. It is light and comfortable and hard-wearing.

Inv. no. 1980–1651
Presented by James North & Sons Ltd

Acid-proof boiler suit
Acid-resistant Dralon (contrAcid)

Suits of this kind are worn by workers in the chemical industry, accumulator factories, bleaching plants, tanneries and elsewhere.
    If acid splashes on to the suit the material has sufficient resistance to give the wearer time to douse the affected area with water.

Inv. no. 1980–1600
Presented by Airguard Ltd

Gas-tight suit in rubber
Rot-proof Diolen coated (on one side) with Neoprene

The Draeger 157 suit is worn with a compressed air breathing apparatus. This example was used by the London Fire Brigade for dealing with incidents involving poisonous chemicals.
    The weight and discomfort of the suit limit the time that it can be reasonably worn to under half an hour, for this reason new procedures using a different kind of suit were introduced in 1980.

Inv. no. 1980–1866   Neg 229/84
Presented by the London Fire Brigade

Gas-tight suit in rubber, Inv no 1980–1866

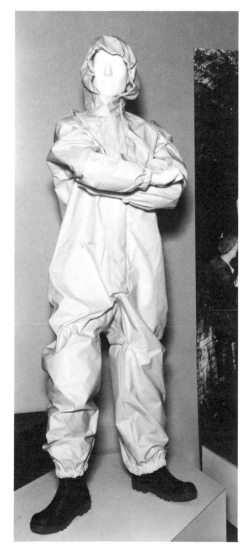

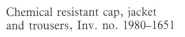

Chemical resistant cap, jacket
and trousers, Inv. no. 1980–1651

Gas-tight suit
Chloro-butyl coated nylon

These suits are worn in situations where toxic vapours may be present, such as repair work in chemical installations.

The material of this example is impervious to all forms of chloride, weak acids, ammonia and all alkalis. It is very easy to put on and there is a gas-tight zip running from the knee to the middle of the hood. The wrists of the suit have gas-tight air locks.

The compressed air breathing apparatus preserved with the suit produces a positive pressure in the face mask. This prevents any inward leakage of outside gas into the mask.

The suit can be ventilated by air from the breathing apparatus; this decreases the risk of inward leakage of gas as well as prolonging the time during which the wearer can work in comfort.

NB. This example has been well-used and would now be considered unfit for further use.

Inv. no. 1981–1460   Neg 230/84
Presented by AGA Spiro Ltd

Gas-tight suit in chlorobutyl coated nylon, Inv no 1981–1460

Gas-tight suit
Polyamide coated in PVC/Nitrile Rubber. Natural rubber boots and gloves

The suit has similar features to suit Inv. no. 1981–1460 except that it has a full face mask built into the hood and does not have a ventilation port. It would also be worn with a self-contained breathing apparatus.

Inv. no. 1982–182
Presented by RFD Mills Equipment Ltd

Forestry worker's chemical spraying suit 1981

The outfit comprises a *Gore-tex* fabric hooded jacket and overtrousers, a face screen and non-toxic particle mask, rubber gloves and neoprene boots. The legs of the trousers which are particularly subject to wear are neoprene coated: neoprene is highly resistant to most chemical pesticides. A pair of special inner socks are supplied with the boots, made from a sandwich of nylon – urethane foam – brushed nylon which allows water vapour from the body to escape but retains body heat.

Note Gore-tex fabric is described in the Foul Weather clothing section.

Inv. no. 1981–1891
Presented by The Forestry Commission

Chemical-resistant combination suit
Neoprene (polychloroprene)

Made from neoprene the suit resists a wide range of chemicals. Extreme changes of temperature do not crack or damage the material. All the seams are stitched and taped. Two layers of neoprene, from elbow to cuff and from knee to ankle, give additional proofing against harmful liquids.

Inv. no. 1982–181
Presented by RFD Mills Equipment Ltd

Nuclear, Biological & Chemical warfare oversuit (Mark 3) 1981
Multi-layer coated fabric

Protective oversuits have been developed because of the possibility that in some future war the combatants might use nuclear, chemical, or biological weapons. This specimen gives protection against all known chemical agents, is flame retardant, self decontaminating and does not make the wearer too hot.

The hooded smock and trousers are made from two layers of material. The inner layer is chemically treated with fluoro compounds and is coated with activated carbon to absorb vapours; the cloth also incorporates a flame retardant. The outer layer is made of nylon and modacrylic yarn to give the best wear resistance possible. This material is showerproof, yet chemical liquids will wet the surface and spread, to evaporate faster. Included in the outfit are cotton inner gloves, neoprene gloves and 'fishtail' neoprene overshoes.

Inv. no. 1983–1157   Neg 215/84
Lent by Compton Webb Group Marketing Ltd

Nuclear, Biological and Chemical warfare suit, Inv no 1983–1157

Antistatic, high voltage and radiation protection

Clothing made from artificial fibres has brought a new problem: the building up of a static electric charge brought about by the friction of the body and the layers of clothing upon one another. An accidental spark discharge of this electricity can damage sensitive micro-electronic circuits, falsify instrument readings, or ignite gases or vapours. For these reasons overalls and other items of clothing have been developed which conduct electricity, allowing any static charge to leak harmlessly away.

Clothing which conducted electricity was also essential if men were to work on a high voltage transmission line in safety without switching off the power. The engineer has to charge himself to the same voltage as the line and the special coveralls developed for this task at first simply incorporated a stainless steel mesh into a woven cotton fabric. Then in 1980–81 a method of blending stainless steel fibres into the material to be spun into thread was devised. For live line work the steel content is 25% but for ordinary antistatic wear good results are achieved with only 1%.

When X-rays were first used many of the operators were harmed by the radiation before the need for proper shielding was understood. Lead-rubber was developed to provide a material which would give a measure of protection from stray radiation and this continues to be used for tabards for the operators. Additional protection is given by measuring the radiation to which operators are exposed and ensuring that this does not exceed a stated figure over a particular period. Film badges were first introduced in the 1930s. Now other types of dosemeters have been brought into use which permit more rapid batch-processing and have a longer (shelf) life. An extension of the badge idea has been the development of dosemeters which measure the exposure of workers to organic solvents.

Live line conducting suit c. 1980
Cotton incorporating stainless steel mesh

This conducting suit is made from cotton fabric incorporating a stainless steel mesh. The main part is a one-piece coverall with an integral hood incorporating a skull protector. The socks and gloves are attached by press-studs bonded to the steel mesh. The suit gives complete low resistance covering to the wearer enabling him to work safely on high voltage transmission lines using a technique devised by Central Electricity Generating Board scientists.

The engineer sits in a chair hung by insulating polypropylene chains from a special crane and is swung out from the transmission line tower. When he approaches the line he clips a lead from the suit to the wire and thus charges himself to the same voltage. With no passage to earth for the electric current the engineer is quite safe and can work on the transmission line. The steel mesh ensures that no difference in voltage can occur between one part of the body and another which would lead to a current flowing.

Inv. no. 1980–1192   Neg 216/84
Lent by Central Electricity Generating Board, South West Region

Live line conducting suit in wool 1980
Natural wool fibre 75% with stainless steel fibres 25%

A new type of conducting suit for use on high voltage lines made from a special woollen fabric containing stainless steel fibres. The suit was developed in 1980 as a result of collaboration between the Central Electricity Generating Board, the International Wool Secretariat and a Belgian weaver.

The fabric is much more flexible than the steel mesh/cotton suit.

Inv. no. 1983–1059
Lent by International Wool Secretariat

Antistatic laboratory coat
Terylene/cotton plus 1% stainless steel fibre, 0.008 mm diameter

This *Permawear* laboratory coat is made from a terylene/cotton fabric which has one percent of stainless steel fibre blended into the spun yarn. The *Bekinox* fibre ensures that any static charge will leak away and since it is part of the yarn, the fabric does not lose its antistatic property after repeated laundering or cleaning.

Inv. no. 1980–1652
Presented by Nicholson's (Overalls) Ltd

Antistatic apron, wristlets and earthing strap

Many microelectronics components can be damaged by even a small discharge of static electricity from the person who may be assembling them into a circuit. Air conditioned clean rooms make the generation of static electricity from clothing more likely. To cancel out this risk an operator will wear this apron, wristlets and wrist strap. Made from a carbon loaded PVC and attached to an earth conductor they ensure that any electric charge immediately leaks harmlessly to earth. As an added precaution the work-bench top, chair-seat and floor may also have similar earthed coverings.

Inv. no. 1981–164
Presented by KAM Circuits Ltd

Radiographers' tabards *
Lead rubber covered by (a) rubberised cotton, (b) nylon

The need to protect those working with X-rays and radioactive substances from the harmful effects of long exposure was not widely appreciated until about 1918. In that year the X-ray and Radium Protection Committee was set up in England and ten years later its recommendations were accepted by all countries.

The conventional protection has always been lead, in one form or another, through which radiation cannot pass. Here it takes the form of lead rubber: a latex/lead powder mixture. These tabards give the same standard degree of protection as lead sheet one half-millimetre thick.

The older tabard is covered by American cloth, the modern one by woven nylon fabric. Their purpose is not to shield the operator from a direct X-ray beam but rather to guard against scattered or stray radiation.

Inv. nos. 1984–83, 87   Neg 271/84
Lent by the Wellcome Museum of the History of Medicine

Standard film badge radiation dosemeter

These were first brought into use in London hospitals in 1937. Radiation affects the strip of photographic film in the badge and when developed this can be used to calculate the amount received by the wearer.

Inv. no. 1981–2174 pt   Neg 217/84
Presented by the National Radiological Protection Board

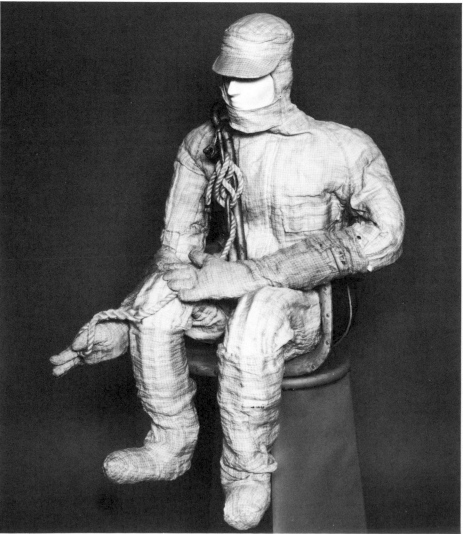

High voltage 'live line' working suit c1980, Inv no 1980–1192

Thermoluminescent radiation dosemeter

This recent development by the National Radiological Protection Board at Harwell uses small discs of lithium fluoride/PTFE. Radiation affects the chemical so that when it is heated a disc will give off minute flashes of light. The amount of light is proportional to the radiation received and can be measured. These dosemeters have the advantage that they remain accurate for relatively long periods of wear, can be re-used after dose measurement and can be processed automatically.

Inv. no. 1981–2174 pt
Presented by the National Radiological
Protection Board   Neg as above

Extremity radiation dosemeter (thermoluminescent)

Used for monitoring at the finger tips.

Inv. no. 1981–2174 pt
Presented by the National Radiological
Protection Board

Neutron radiation dosemeter

This uses nucleur emulsion film which records photographically the tracks produced by exposure to neutrons. The tracks are counted under a microscope and are proportional to the neutron dose received by the badge wearer.

Inv. no. 1981–2174   Neg as above
Presented by the National Radiological
Protection Board

Organic solvent vapour monitoring badge

Many synthetic paints, glues and cleaning fluids give off vapours when being applied. The solvents are based on organic chemicals and prolonged exposure to these vapours can be harmful. Therefore workers using or manufacturing these substances wear sampler badges like this ORSA 5 type. The plastic badge holds a glass tube of activated charcoal sealed at each end, the organic vapours can diffuse through the seals and are then absorbed by the charcoal. After use the tube is sent to a laboratory and the amount of vapour absorbed is determined by methods such as gas chromatography.

Certain types of chemical vapour can be monitored by the colour change in chemicals carried in similar badges; the exposure is calculated by measuring the depth of colour.

Inv. no. 1982–544   Neg 217/84
Presented by Draeger Safety Ltd

Radiation dosemeter badges and organic solvent vapour dosemeter,
Inv nos 1981–2174, 1982–554

Radiographer's lead-rubber tabard.
Inv no 1984–83

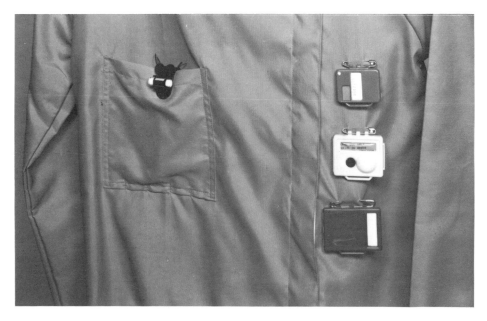

Clean room wear and disposable garments

The use of special clothing for hygienic reasons has long been established in the medical profession and in food preparation industries, but in the 1930s a new group of workers became concerned with especially clean clothing – those in the photographic film making industry. The new projectors for the giant cinemas then being built brought a need for very fine grain emulsion which would given clear pictures at great magnification. During the making and processing of such film the slightest contamination would produce large blemishes when projected and so clean rooms were introduced, with special dress for the workers. The problem re-occurred in the electronics industry in the 1950s when special valves for submarine telephone cables were first being built and subsequently as electronic circuitry became further and further miniaturised. Non-linting clothes which retain the tiny skin particles our bodies shed every day have to be worn and workrooms are supplied with filtered and conditioned air.

Clothes made from paper first appeared in Britain in the last century and reappeared in the 1950s. Nowadays a number of non-woven fabrics are available and can be made up into clothing sufficiently cheap to be thrown away or destroyed when contaminated. The term 'non-woven' is used since the cloth is produced by pressing and sticking fibres together, often with chemical bonding agents, rather than by traditional warp and weft procedures.

Clean Room wear in antistat *Celon* 1980

A one-piece coverall and boot protectors.

Inv. no. 1980–1562
Presented by Multifabs Ltd

Clean room wear in ceramic terylene 1980

A two-piece suit with a separate hood. Ceramic terylene is made by passing the woven fabric through heated pressure rollers which close up the interstices in the weave.

Inv. no. 1980–1563
Presented by Multifabs Ltd

Pharmaceutical aseptic area wear 1982

A one-piece combination suit of polyester with hood, disposable face mask, surgical gloves and plastic-soled canvas sandals. Used by workers filling ampoules with drug solutions. After use the clothing is sterilised in an autoclave.

Inv. no. 1982–158
Presented by Burroughs Wellcome Pharmaceutical Co. Ltd

Pharmaceutical preparation area wear 1982

A one-piece combination suit of ceramic terylene, with hood, disposable face mask, safety spectacles, surgical gloves and plastic-soled canvas shoes. Used in areas where every precaution is taken to keep particles from contaminating the product, bacteria will automatically be eliminated when the product is sterilised.

Inv. no. 1982–159
Presented by Burroughs Wellcome Pharmaceutical Co. Ltd

Clean room outfit in anti-stat *Celon* 1960

This outfit was formerly issued to staff at what was then the GPO laboratories at Martlesham Heath. It comprises: pork pie hat, one-piece coverall, nylon gloves with polyurethane finger tips and shoes with antistatic inner soles.

Inv. no. 1982–165
Presented by British Telecom Research Laboratories

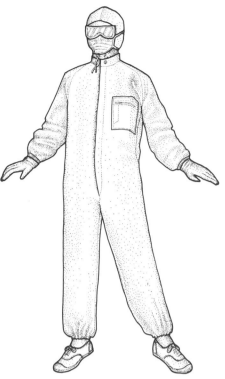

Pharmaceutical worker's outfit, inv. no. 1982–158

Clean room outfit 1960, Inv. no. 1982–165

Clean room clothing 1980

These examples were in use at Mullard Ltd micro-electronics factory. They comprise ceramic terylene jacket, two antistatic nylon jackets, an antistatic *Celon* jacket, three peaked nylon caps, two peaked nylon caps with snoods.

Inv. no. 1983–8
Presented by Mullard Ltd

Clean room snood and hood 1981

A terylene net snood with ceramic terylene brow band, and a ceramic terylene vizor hood.

Inv. no. 1981–1930
Presented by Contamination Control Apparel Ltd

Clean room plastic sandals 1980

Inv. no. 1980–1566
Presented by Multifabs Ltd

Autoclave bag 1980

A ceramic terylene bag used to hold clean garments ready for sterilising.

Inv. no. 1980–1568
Presented by Multifabs Ltd

Surgeon's gown 1980

Made from a scrim laminate non-woven fabric; a cellulose tissue/nylon gauze/cellulose tissue sandwich.

Inv. no. 1981–28
Presented by Luxan Medex Ltd

Two nursing gowns 1980

One long, one short sleeve gown made from a two-ply paper-based wadding.

Inv. no. 1981–29
Presented by Luxan Medex Ltd

Disposable mob cap 1980

Inv. no. 1981–30
Presented by Luxan Medex Ltd

Disposable theatre face mask 1980

Inv. no. 1981–31
Presented by Luxan Medex Ltd

Disposable two ply ward mask 1980

Inv. no. 1981–32
Presented by Luxan Medex Ltd

Disposable aprons 1981

Thin PVC aprons which can be worn for a few hours and afterwards are cheap enough to throw away. For hospital use the two sides are different colours so the wearer can avoid any risk of cross infection should they remove the apron for a few minutes.

Inv. no. 1981–33
Presented by Luxan Medex Ltd

Non-woven disposable hospital theatre tunic and trousers 1981

The *Barrier* operating-theatre wear is made from crepe finish paper.

Inv. no. 1981–431
Presented by Johnson and Johnson Ltd

Non-woven disposable surgical gown 1981

Made from crepe finish paper.

Inv. no. 1981–433
Presented by Johnson and Johnson Ltd

Non-woven disposable hospital theatre dress 1981

Made from the same material as Inv. no. 1981–431

Inv. no. 1981–432
Presented by Johnson and Johnson Ltd

Non-woven disposable hoods 1981

Intended for head coverings in hospitals, made from regenerated cellulose xanthate bonded with vinyl acrylic resin.

Inv. no. 1981–434
Presented by Johnson and Johnson Ltd

Non-Woven, Hospital patient's cap 1981

Made from the same material as Inv. no. 1981–434.

Inv. no. 1981–437
Presented by Johnson and Johnson Ltd

Non-woven disposable hoods for hospital use 1981

Made from the same material as Inv. no. 1981–434; in balaclava style.

Inv. no. 1981–435
Presented by Johnson and Johnson Ltd

Non-woven disposable cap for nurses 1981

Made from the same material as Inv. no. 1981–434.

Inv. no. 1981–436
Presented by Johnson and Johnson Ltd

Disposable, tie-on surgical mask 1981

Inv. no. 1981–438
Presented by Johnson and Johnson Ltd

Non-woven disposable coverall and bootcovers 1981

This is made from *Tyvek*, a spunbonded olefin, and intended either for clean room use or in situations where dirt or contamination makes it necessary to destroy the clothing after use. The coverall fabric is strong enough to be worn several times before disposal is necessary.

Inv. no. 1981–457
Presented by Greenham Tool Co

Non-woven disposable mob cap 1981

Made from the paper based fabric used for Inv. no. 1981–434.

Inv. no. 1981–599
Presented by Kanga Hospital Products Ltd

Disposable opaque polythene overshoes 1981

Inv. no. 1981–600
Presented by Kanga Hospital Products Ltd

Disposable 3 ply overshoes 1981

Made from a cellulose tissue/polythene/tissue sandwich.

Inv. no. 1981–601
Presented by Kanga Hospital Products Ltd

Chef's paper toque

Traditionally the tall chef's hat has been made from starched linen or cotton. This example is cheap enough for disposal as soon as it becomes soiled and is made from strong white paper with an embossed linen finish. The crown is pierced to allow for ventilation and the sweatband is highly absorbent.

Inv. no. 1982–1793
Presented by Pal Wear Disposables

Disposable paper forage caps

Made from a strong, tear-resistant creped paper. One cap has a lightweight tissue crown the other a non-woven mesh crown.

Inv. no. 1982–1794
Presented by Pal Wear Disposables

Disposable paper bonnet and nurses cap

These two hats are made from a strong linen embossed card and are supplied packed flat. Both can be quickly folded into shape, the bonnet using tabs and slots and the cap a single stud to secure the folds.

Inv. nos. 1982–1795, 1796
Presented by Pal Wear Disposables

Non-woven overshoes, oversleeves, gauntlets and overall

Made from the same material as Inv. no. 1981–457, intended for clean room or hospital use.

Inv. no. 1984–184
Presented by Strentex Fabrics Ltd

Non-woven headscarf, cap with snood, mob cap, oversleeves and teeshirt

Made from the same material as Inv. no. 1981–434, intended for clean room or hospital use.

Inv. no. 1984–185
Presented by Strentex Fabrics Ltd

General industrial outfits

This section contains outfits not readily catalogued elsewhere.

Shinglers at Brindley Ford in the early 20th century, see Inv no 1984–212
(Courtesy Staffordshire County Museum, Shugborough)

Shingler's protective wear nineteenth century (replicas)

Shingling was the process of working a mass of white-hot iron and slag under a steam hammer. The men needed special protection from the molten slag and sparks which were flung in all directions as the hammer hit the ball. Shinglers wore ordinary rough working trousers, a woollen vest and cotton shirt, with a sweat rag about the neck. Over these clothes they wore a heavy leather apron with sheet-iron shin guards and boot covers strapped to their legs. On their heads they wore a simple cotton skull cap and a wire gauze face screen. The shin and foot protectors, apron, face screen and skull cap are replicas of those preserved by Shugborough Museum.

Inv. no. 1984–212
Made in the Museum Workshops

North Sea oil rig worker's outfit 1980

The North Sea oil rig worker faces conditions which require special clothing if he is to work efficiently and safely. Exposure to very cold and wet situations is coupled with the need to protect him against possible accidents such as fire and falling objects. The outfit comprises: hard hat; quilted undersuit; fire-resistant overall in high visibility orange; waterproof over-trousers with aluminised lining; waterproof anorak; antistatic boots with oil resistant soles and fur lining.

Inv. no. 1980–1193
Neg 1106/82/5, 1106/82/10 (undersuit only), 194/82
Presented by British Petroleum Development Ltd

Chef's outfit 1980

The familiar chef's costume, over about five hundred years, finally achieved this form in the early 1900s. Although fashion has controlled some features – notably the style of hat – the outfit has practical advantages.

Hat (or toque), neckerchief, double breasted jacket with split cuffs, checked trousers and an apron.

Inv. no. 1981–824
Presented by Alexandra Workwear Ltd

Coalminer's outfit 1980

The National Coal Board issues outfits like this specimen to all its underground workers. It comprises: safety helmet with cap lamp and battery, high visibility orange overalls, boots with reinforced toecaps and ankles and non-slip soles, rubber knee pads, duffle coat with

reflective strips on sleeves and shoulders, and gloves. Each miner also carries a self-rescuer canister on his belt. The filter mask it contains extracts dust and moisture and changes poisonous carbon monoxide into the less harmful carbon dioxide giving a man time to escape from an area suddenly flooded with carbon monoxide.

Inv. no. 1983–867
Lent by National Coal Board, Exhibitions Department

American miner's jacket and trousers 1978

Designed by a group at Cornell University, sponsored by AMOCO and using fabric provided by the International Wool Secretariat.

Miners tested the garments for ten months during 1978. They found that the overalls lasted about three times longer than those made from cotton blends and

they particularly liked the velcro cuff-fastenings and the reflective sleeve bands and triangle on the back of the jacket which added to their comfort and safety.

Inv. no. 1983–1058
Lent by the International Wool Secretariat

Mine rescue outfit 1950*

Mine rescue teams have to be able to contend with many adverse conditions such as lack of oxygen, confined spaces, dampness and low visibility. However, until relatively recent times the outfit and equipment used by a mine rescuer had changed very little since the turn of this century.
1950 outfit
Mine rescue personnel of this period were equipped with a Proto MkIV breathing apparatus, protective helmet, knee pads, cap lamp and power pack worn over flannel collarless shirt, tweed knee breeches, woollen stockings and ordinary work boots.

Inv. no. 1951–663   Neg. 231/84
Presented by Siebe Gorman and Co. Ltd

Mine rescue outfit 1950, Inv no 1951–663

North Sea oil rig worker's outfit 1980,
Inv no 1980–1193

JOHN FREEMAN

JOHN FREEMAN

Sewer flusher's outfit

In the course of his daily work the sewer flusher encounters damp and dirty surroundings. The outfit worn is intended to make his work as comfortable as possible. It comprises: cotton overalls, thigh high rubber wading boots, rubber gloves, plastic safety helmet, and safety belt.

Inv. no. 1980–1727   Neg 1095/82/4
Presented by the Thames Water Authority

Shotblaster's outfit 1980

Industrial shotblasting, a process for cleaning heavily corroded metal components, has been in use since the late nineteenth century. Crushed grit is blown at high speed through a gun directed at the corroded metal. Though usually performed within a metal chamber, the process is sometimes performed outdoors.

This outfit was extensively used by Mr David Fleming and consists of a heavy canvas jacket and trousers, with the additional protection of leather apron, gloves, sturdy boots, and a metal, air-fed helmet. The compressor that forces grit through the gun also supplies fresh air to the helmet, thus ensuring that the workman will not inhale any of the dust and metal particles flying around him.

Inv. no. 1981–416
Presented by Impact Finishers Ltd

Shotblaster's outfit 1980

An unused outfit consisting of a zip-up, one-piece canvas suit, a heavy duty neoprene apron, a rubber-covered air-fed helmet, reinforced rubber gauntlets and moulder's boots. The boots have a quick-release mechanism on the heel.

Inv. no. 1980–1588
Presented by Jelaco Ltd

Explosive ordnance disposal suit Mk2
'Kevlar' with rigid ceramic armour inserts.

Designed to give personnel protection whilst disarming small improvised explosive devices (and other ordnance), this two-piece suit and visored helmet gives almost fullcover protection against fragments but also provides some defence against blast and flame.

Most of the suit is made from *Kevlar* and rigid ceramic plates are slipped into pockets at the front of the jacket for added protection. A two way communication system is fitted into the helmet. The whole suit weighs about 24 kg (51 lbs).

Inv. no. 1983–1078
Lent by the Ministry of Defence

Asbestos dust protective suit

Ceramic terylene

The discovery of the harmful effects of even minute amounts of asbestos dust led to the development of special clothing for handling the substance. This one-piece coverall conforms to the Asbestos Research Council's (ARC) recommendations. It is made from ceramic terylene, a fibre which dust cannot cling to, nor pass through the woven fabric.

Inv. no. 1980–1564
Presented by Multifabs Ltd

Explosive ordnance disposal suit
Inv. no. 1983–1078

Sewer flusher's outfit, Inv no 1980–1727

JOHN FREEMAN

Forestry worker's tree felling outfit 1981

The Forestry Commission supply these outfits to their workers together with others for general work and for chemical spraying. The tree-fellers wear a standard safety helmet with wire face screen and ear muffs, anorak with detachable hood in polyurethane-coated nylon, trousers in the same material with pockets in the legs for chain-saw guard pads, leather mitts with the right hand glove having an index finger and thumb and the left having a padded back, the boots have safety toecaps and a ballistic nylon tongue. The chain saw guards with these specimens are pads of 28 layers of knitted nylon but a new design is now available which contains 4 layers of *Kevlar* cloth (see Inv. no. 1982–665). Rubber boots and waterproof over-trousers are also supplied.

Inv. no. 1981–1890
Presented by The Forestry Commission

Forestry worker's general work outfit 1981

Comprises thornproof, waxed cotton jacket (with separate hood) and trousers, smock top in heavy cotton, safety boots, wire handling gloves in riggers pattern with cotton backs and leather palms and cuffs. A first aid kit is standard issue with this clothing and an example is held with these specimens.

Inv. no. 1981–1892
Presented by The Forestry Commission

Mineral oil protective suit
Front: polyurethane coated knitted nylon
Back: polyester cotton

The *Jackson* suit was specially designed by Multifabs, in conjunction with Rolls-Royce, Derby. It protects personnel who work alongside machines that spray mineral oil, a likely cancer-forming substance.
    The front of the suit is made of *Multithene* (first produced in 1965) which is oil resistant.
    For the suit to be comfortable when worn for long periods the body must 'breathe', therefore the back of the suit is made of polyester cotton.

Inv. no. 1980–1565
Presented by Multifabs Ltd

Non-woven acid resistant disposable coverall
Acid-resistant suit in black Tyvek, *coated with polyethylene*

A disposable outfit made from *Tyvek*, a tough durable material made from spinning very fine (0.005 mm diameter) polyethylene fibres and bonding them by heat and pressure. *Tyvek* is a very versatile material – it can be made stiff and paper-like or soft and drapeable. It combines many of the properties of fabrics and paper.

Inv. no. 1982–741.
Presented by D H J Industries (UK) Ltd.

Disposable coverall
Polypropylene

The garment is intended for use in the chemical, pharmaceutical and aerospace industries. The polypropylene material has very low fluid and dust absorption characteristics which ensures that little, or no dust (or liquid) contaminant is transferred outside the working area. These characteristics also ensure that washing down (where necessary) does not create a fabric breakdown. The fabric is vapour permeable making it comfortable to wear.

Inv. no. 1983–165
Presented by the Fire Service Supply Co

Laboratory Coat

This coat's design was based on recommendations for laboratory wear made in the Howie report† of 1979. It is made of white polyester cotton with wrapover front, side fastening with press studs, high neck, long sleeves with close fitting cuffs.

Inv. no. 1980–159
Presented by Multifabs Ltd

† Code of practice for the prevention of infection clinical laboratories and post mortem rooms. D.H.S.S. ISBN 0113204647

General protective wear

This section includes industrial helmets, spectacles, goggles and face screens, ear protectors, gloves, boots and shoes, protective waistcoats, aprons and leg and arm protectors.

The use of protective headgear at work was confined to a comparatively small number of industries in this country until quite recently. In the eighteenth and nineteenth centuries miners and quarrymen made use of leather and lime-washed or shellaced felt hats to protect their heads, although their use was not universal. The return of steel helmets in the 1914–18 war seems to have led to the adoption of metal helmets (usually aluminium), particularly in the oil and construction industries in America between the wars, but not until about 1945 was there any encouragement for wearing industrial helmets in this country. In mining, helmet-wearing finally became compulsory in 1943, and gradually since then legislation has made the provision of head protection necessary in more and more industries. Vehicle-users' helmets evolved from soft leather flying helmets, the army introducing hard-shelled helmets for despatch riders in the 1940s. The motor racing governing bodies made them compulsory in the 1950s and, after a long campaign for voluntary adoption, legislation compelled motor cyclists to wear them from 1973 onwards.

Early face and eye protection from flying sparks, splinters or abrasive particles was given by fine wire gauze made up into masks or goggles. When laminated and toughened glasses were introduced in this century their general adoption was in part limited by their comparatively high cost. The invention of the polycarbonate range of plastics brought costs down to the point where eye protection is now widely provided.

Often the introduction of protective wear owes as much to general realization of hazards as to a new invention; hearing protection is a case in point. The damage to hearing from continuous exposure to industrial noise was reported on as early as the eighteenth century in medical documents. The first protectors were invented in 1915 for the use of artillerymen and research done in 1939 led to improvements in air crew helmets. It was only in the 1950s that campaigning began to persuade workers to protect their hearing, with a range of hearing protectors being developed since then.

Gloves and mittens have been worn for many centuries and for hard wear and handling rough or thorny material leather was first choice. Rubber gloves made by a dipping process appeared in 1878, worn by surgeons to protect their hands from the carbolic acid used as a disinfectant. The first plastic gloves were produced in 1947 and the dipping and curing method of manufacture patented in 1948. Artificial fibres intended to replace asbestos in heat-resistant gloves have been produced in recent years. There is now a very wide variety of gloves of all kinds and materials for use in industry, the home and sport.

Specialised boots and shoes have appeared many times in the history of clothing and the eighteenth and nineteenth centuries produced a range of designs. The wooden-soled clog in various shapes and forms has found many industrial uses, for the soles protect against heat, or cold, or damp underfoot conditions and resist many chemicals much better than leather. Boots with an internal steel toecap were first brought to Britain from America in 1938 and nine years later manufacture under licence began here. Rubber boots are now so common that it is forgotten that their use in industry was fairly restricted until the 1920s and even then leather sea boots were recommended in preference to rubber. Natural rubber footwear was made by the South American Indians possibly as early as the thirteenth century and was first sold in the United States in about 1830. The destruction of rubber plantations during the 1939–45 war accelerated the research into the production of synthetic rubbers and most protective footwear now uses synthetic rather than natural rubber.

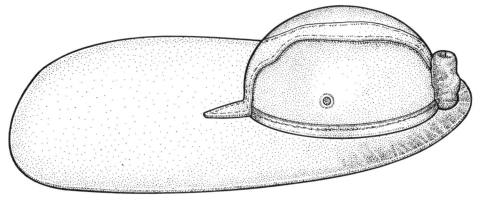

Nineteenth century shaft sinker's helmet, inv. no. 1981–1651

Mine-shaft sinker's helmet nineteenth century*

Typical of the leather helmets used when sinking new shafts, with the brim extended into a long flap at the back giving protection from water dripping from the roof. This examples comes from South Northumberland.

Inv. no. 1981–1651	Neg 1584/83,
Purchased	195/82
	with Inv. no. 1983–824

Miner's skull cap and lamp c. 1925*

Many miners wore only rudimentary head protection and some none at all. This canvas skull cap with its attached lamp was sold by Messrs. Oldham & Son Ltd. during the 1920s.

Inv. no. 1925–683
Presented by Oldham & Son Ltd

Vulcanised fibre miner's helmet 1950s*

This design was widely used after helmet wearing was made compulsory in 1943 (the miners had to buy their own at that time).

Inv. no. 1981–1653 pt
Purchased

Resin-bonded fabric miner's helmet 1950s*

This *Texflex* helmet is one of the early examples of a plastic being used for a protective industrial hat.

Inv. no. 1981–1653 pt   Neg 1582/83
Purchased

Miner's aluminium helmet 1982

Being made of non-ferrous metal there is no risk of sparking if knocked. The helmet is cap-shaped.

Inv. no. 1982–171
Presented by MSA (Britain) Ltd

Motorcycle helmet 1957*

Made from compressed cork and carried on a cradle of straps, this is typical of helmets used at this time.

Inv. no. 1981–2082   Neg 913/83
Presented by R. Aylward Esq

Open face helmet 1980

The '*Pinto*' helmet is intended for light motorcycle or moped riders. Made in a thermoplastic and padded throughout it conforms to BS 5361. The concept of a hard shell completely padded inside, instead of the shell being supported on a cradle of straps, resulted from work carried out by the Road Research Laboratory which led to a new British Standard in 1956.

Inv. no. 1980–981
Presented by Kangol Helmets Ltd

Full-face helmet 1980

In the 1960s competition riders began wearing helmets which extended down over the cheeks and round over the jaws completely enclosing the face and they soon came into general use. This *Phil Read* helmet is made in fibreglass to BS 2496 (of 1977) with a fully padded interior and special cheek pads. The visor seats onto a rubber edging.

Inv. no. 1980–982
Presented by Kangol Helmets Ltd

Miner's helmet, resin-bonded fabric 1950s, Inv no 1981–1653

Cork based motorcyclist's helmet 1957, Inv no 1981–2082

Racing car driver's helmet 1980

Driving helmets were made compulsory in races in 1952. The first designs were similar to motorcycle helmets, now the full face cover is standard. This example is hand contact moulded using a gelcoat, chopped glass fibre, strand mat and a woven roving cloth. The helmet exceeds the requirements of BS 2495FR.

The interior of the shell is moulded expanded polystyrene bead with polyester foam and a flame retardant foam backed lining material trimmed with leather. The visor is double thickness 2 mm polycarbonate with a swivelling action and stop points to prevent contact with the shell.

The life support intake nozzle fitted to the helmet is connected to an air bottle in the car's cockpit. In a crash if a fire breaks out a press button system delivers pure air for 30 seconds to the driver; adequate time for him to undo his seat belts and escape from the car.

Inv. no. 1980–1421
Presented by Thetford Moulded Products Ltd

Driving helmet shells

(a) Fibreglass. 20% of the helmet has not been treated with resin exposing the five layers of matting used in its construction.
(b) Polycarbonate. The example in the collection has been used in BSI penetration tests and shows, clearly, two such impacts.

Inv. no. (a) 1982–146 (b) 1982–147
Presented by Euro-Helmets Ltd

Motorcycle helmet with hinged chin guard

In order to be effective a full-face motorcycle helmet must fit closely to the head. Should the wearer of such a helmet injure his jaw in an accident removing the helmet could cause further damage. The *BMW System Helmet* has the chin guard section hinged making it easier to put on and take off. The transparent visor has four alternative positions (each locked) and needs only one hand to operate it. The chin section of the helmet can be easily removed converting it into an open helmet.

Safety standard certificates have been issued for this helmet in West Germany and the United States of America. Introduction of the helmet into Britain has been delayed pending the establishment of a British Standard test procedure.

Inv. no. 1984–90
Presented by BMW (GB) Ltd

Metropolitan Police helmets (sectioned)

The familiar policeman's helmet developed as part of his distinctive uniform. In its original form it offered little protection, for many years being made up on a cork base (example 'A').

After many policemen had been injured by stones and bricks in the street riots in Notting Hill the Metropolitan Police Clothing Branch was asked to strengthen the helmet. The mark 5 design (example 'B') has a rigid ABS (Acrylonitrile-Butadiene-Styrene) shell.

Other experimental designs, including a Woman Police Officer's hat, were being tried out in 1982–83.

Inv. no. 1983–604, 605   Neg 175/84
Presented by the Metropolitan Police

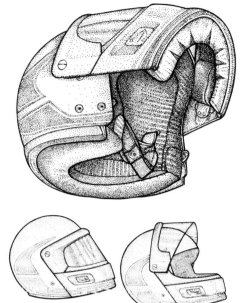

Motorcycle helmet, Inv. no. 1984–90

Police riot helmet

This type of helmet has been adopted by overseas police forces to give total head protection to their men engaged on riot control duty. The helmet is moulded in glass-reinforced plastic material and weighs 5kg. A padded cradle and cup-shaped chin strap ensure that it fits securely and comfortably on the wearer's head. A visor clips to the front of the helmet and leaves a small air space to prevent misting over.

Inv. no. 1983–1080
Lent by Bristol Composite Materials Engineering Ltd, Avonmouth

Fireman's helmet, 1977

Early firemen's helmets were made of leather. Brass helmets were introduced into the Metropolitan Fire Brigade in 1866 and were soon adopted by other brigades. Later these brass helmets were found to be dangerous, owing to the possibility of the fireman coming into contact with bared electric wiring and in 1937 the London Fire Brigade adopted the cork helmets, of which this is an example. It is constructed of 3-ply cork covered in flameproof cotton and finished with acid-resistant and heat-resisting enamel.

Inv. no. 1982–961
Presented by the London Fire Brigade

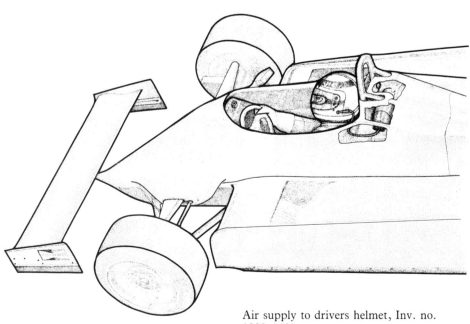

Air supply to drivers helmet, Inv. no. 1980–1421

Shotblaster's helmet 1981, with air heater unit

This helmet is made from fibreglass with a coating of abrasive resistant paint on the outside. The polycarbonate visor has a detachable metal gauze screen to give additional protection when heavy shot or chopped piano wire is in use. This design should be compared with the traditional rubber covered shotblast helmet and the metal helmet also in the collection (see entries for shotblaster's suits).

Air is driven into the reservoir between the helmet's inner and outer shells, and emerges by vents fitted to the inner shell. In cold conditions the *Vortemp* air heater can be fitted to the air hose. The compressed air is fed into a chamber through tangential slots to create a miniature cyclone with a very high number of revolutions per minute in the generator. From the generator the swirling air passes through a hole and up into the vortex tube. As the air moves up this tube the outer portion becomes hot and is tapped off by a restriction at the top of the tube and fed into the air line to the helmet.

Inv. no. 1981–598   Neg 178/84
Presented by 3M (United Kingdom) PLC

Glass fibre ventilated helmet

The *Harwell* helmet was developed in conjunction with the UK Atomic Energy Authority and was used at Harwell to give protection from liquid and metallic sodium. The glass fibre is bonded with a self extinguishing polyester resin and has a *Triplex* toughened glass visor. Two circular vents under the 'chin' allow air to flow over the face and out through the vent on the crown of the helmet. The shoulder cape is in leather which is resistant to hot sodium.

Inv. no. 1982–1767
Presented by Atomic Energy Research Establishment, Harwell

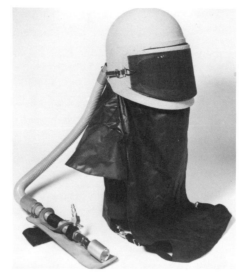

Shotblaster's helmet 1981 with *Vortemp* air heater unit, Inv no 1981–598

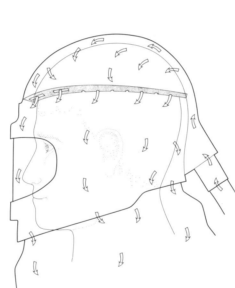

Section through a shot blaster's helmet showing air flow, inv. no. 1981–598

Glass fibre ventilated helmet 1981

This *Updraft Mk10* helmet is a development of the *Harwell*. The larger anti-mist visor is in polycarbonate, the lower ventilation ports are baffled and the shoulder cape is in acid-resistant PVC. The helmet can be worn for long periods in comfort while giving good protection from falling liquids or upward splashes.

Inv. no. 1982–184
Presented by R F D Inflatables Ltd

Lightweight bump cap

In polypropylene copolymer to BS 4033 and intended for use in the food industry where the cap must be frequently sterilised. Not intended to give protection from falling objects but against accidental knocks.

Inv. no. 1980–776
Presented by Safety Products Ltd

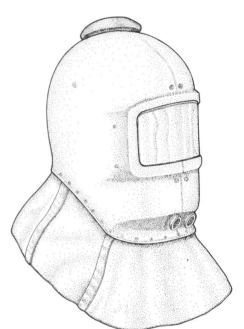

Glassfibre ventilated helmet, Inv. no. 1982–1767

Metropolitan Police helmets with ABS shell (left) and cork shell (right), Inv nos 1983–604, 605

Weatherproof bump cap

For plumbers, mechanics or aircraft workers. The outer cover is in PVC with an inner shell of injection moulded ABS (Acrylonitrile-Butadiene-Styrene), foam lined; conforms to BS 4033.

Inv. no. 1980–1422
Presented by Thetford Moulded Products Ltd

Glass fibre one-piece shell safety helmet

Compression moulded (*Centurion 200*) giving maximum protection in high temperature areas such as foundries and rolling mills.

Inv. no. 1980–1423
Presented by Thetford Moulded Products Ltd

High density polyethylene safety helmet

Injection moulded, low dome shell (*Centurion 400*) for general purpose use.

Inv. no. 1980–1424
Presented by Thetford Moulded Products Ltd

High density polyethylene safety helmet

Injection moulded shell (*Centurion 700*) for construction and general site use. A rain channel is incorporated in the moulding and it is suitable for use in temperatures down to −20°C.

Inv. no. 1980–1425
Presented by Thetford Moulded Products Ltd

High density polyethylene low dome safety helmet

Injection moulded shell (*Centurion 1125*) designed to give protection against sideways crushing forces and electrical resistivity up to 440 volts. This helmet is also suitable for low temperature use. Side slots make it possible to add accessories such as ear defenders, face screens etc., without the need to drill through the shell. A face screen with carrier is included with the helmet.

Inv. no. 1980–1426, 1427
Presented by Thetford Moulded Products Ltd

Chinese construction worker's hat 1981

This protective hat made from woven cane was purchased in Nanking, China, where such hats are widely used by building site workers. A simple cradle of straps is riveted to the hat to support it on the head. While not as effective as the modern

Western plastic helmets the resilience of the canework gives some protection against knocks or blows from light, falling objects.

Inv. no. 1983–824
Neg 195/82 with Inv. no. 1981–1651
Neg 1343/82 with a tin miner's hat and a pre-1788 miner's hat
Neg 1102/82/8
Lent by Mrs R M Thomas

Eskimo snow goggles*

Having no access to glass, the Eskimos made primitive goggles out of wood as a protection against snow blindness, caused by the glare of the sun on snow. A narrow slit restricts the amount of light reaching the eyes and a short "peak" above the slit gives some protection from direct sunlight.

Wellcome no. A 300753   Neg 259/84
Lent by the Wellcome Museum of the History of Medicine

Eskimo snow goggles,
Wellcome no A300753

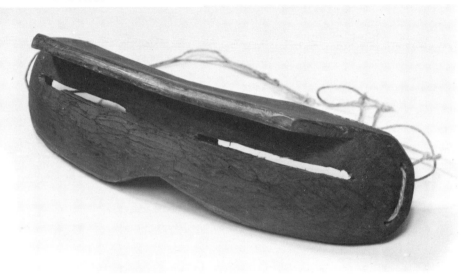

Chinese construction worker's hat 1981, in woven cane, Inv no 1983–824

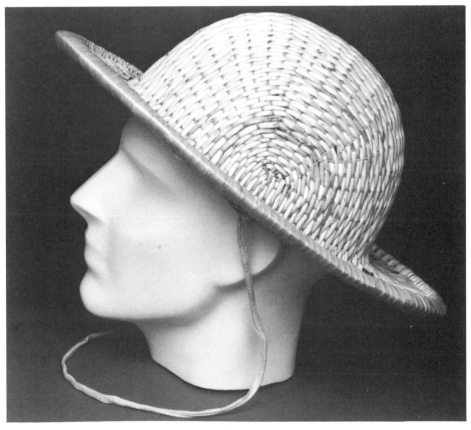

Goggles used on the Nares expedition to the Arctic in 1875*

Coloured lenses were made almost as soon as spectacles were introduced in Europe and this pair were used by the ship's carpenter.

Wellcome no. A651472
Lent by the Wellcome Museum of the History of Medicine

Occiombras (Calkins patent) c. 1871*

Simple cotton net eyeshields like this specimen were sold under this fanciful name as a protection for the eyes against sun and wind and are listed in a contemporary catalogue at a cost of 6s 6d.

Wellcome no. A651418
Lent by the Wellcome Museum of the History of Medicine

Tank driver's eye protectors 1917*

The early tanks had quite a large opening in front of the driver for him to see through. These steel eye shields gave protection against shell splinters or shrapnel; some examples have chain mesh hanging from the bottom as protection for the face. The shields are curved and hinged to fit the face with narrow slits in the dished portions over the eyes. A fabric strap holds them in place on the head.

Wellcome No. A652303   Neg 260/84
Lent by the Wellcome Museum of the History of Medicine

Grinder's goggles c. 1920

The use of small wire mesh cups as eye protectors was fairly common in the 19th century; these goggles have glass discs set into them to give improved vision.

Inv. no. 1981–84
Transferred from the Museum Workshops

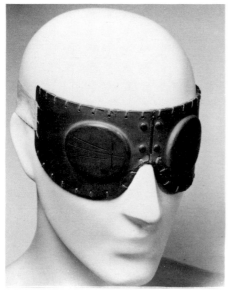

Tar sprayer's goggles

Originally used in the early years of this century by road menders working for Wiltshire County Council Highways Department. The goggles have small glass lenses in metal frames with canvas eye cups.

Inv. no. 1984–248
Presented by Wiltshire County Council

Safety spectacles with polycarbonate lenses

The *Armamax* spectacles are made to B.S.2092 and withstand grade 2 impact, they can be supplied with lenses ground to the wearer's own prescription.

Inv. no. 1980–772
Presented by Safety Products Ltd

Safety spectacles with polycarbonate lenses

The *COIL* spectacles are designed to give greater depth of protection without the need to wear a face screen, they are to BS 2092 grade 2 impact.

Inv. no. 1981–454
Presented by Combined Optical Industries Ltd

Safety goggles

The *Vistamax* goggles have twin polycarbonate lenses, rather like double glazing, to overcome misting. When it is damaged the outer lens can be replaced without the need to discard the complete set. This pair also have anti-splash ventilators fitted. They are to BS 2092 grade 1 impact.

Inv. no. 1980–773
Presented by Safety Products Ltd

Tank driver's goggles 1917
Wellcome no A652303

Polycarbonate face screen

The *Clearways* face screen would be used where there is a risk of harmful liquids or particles being thrown up into the face. In some industries tinted and half-silvered screens shield the wearer from heat and glare. This example is to BS 2092 grade 2 impact and chemical resistant.

Inv. no. 1980–774
Presented by Safety Products Ltd

Dust respirator goggles

These acetate lens goggles have been designed to be worn with dust respirators. The acetate impregnated lens (to BS 2092 impact grade 2) prevent fogging and the snug-fit flange ensures a close fit to facial contours. The wide vision frame enables the goggles to be worn over normal spectacles.

Inv. no. 1981–465
Presented by Martindale Protection Ltd

Furnaceman's spectacles 1981

Metal-framed tinted spectacles with side shields to cut glare from all directions and having a removable leather casing on the nose piece to prevent it getting too hot. The side shields are hinged for easy storage.

Inv. no. 1982–169
Presented by British American Optical Co Ltd

Half-tinted spectacles 1981

The half-tinted sections are hinged at the top and can be swung out of the way. Hinged gauze side shields keep out grit or spatter.

Inv. no. 1982–170
Presented by British American Optical Co Ltd

Furnaceman's half-tinted spectacles, inv. no. 1982–170

Safety spectacles with side shields 1983

These 'Spec E' safety spectacles give similar protection to that afforded by goggles with a minimum of facial contact. The side arm and its hinge permit individual adjustment and give improved vision as there is no vertical bar where lens and sideshield meet. The sideshield hinge allows replacement of the shields within seconds. If the worker is exceptionally active he can fit an elastic headband to the side arms to prevent the spectacles slipping off.

Inv. no. 1983–371
Lent by Rely Upon Protection

Protective spectacles with side shields 1982

These protective spectacles have nylon frames with adjustable side arms and lens position. The side shields are acetate and the lenses of polycarbonate.

Inv. no. 1983–120
Presented by Birch-Stigmat Group Ltd

Welder's face screen 1981

The intense light emitted by welding arc or flame will quickly cause permanent damage to the eyes unless a tinted filter is used. The colour of the filter and its density varies according to the welding method being used. In past years most welders used goggles or held screens in front of their faces which had a small inset filter glass. The hand-held screen has largely given way to those carried on helmets or headbands.

This *Prota* welding screen is in vulcanised fibre giving good protection against metal particles and sparks. The dark green filter glass is pivoted and can be raised leaving a clear glass permitting easy inspection of the completed work. The plate-holder and the headbands are of nylon.

Inv. no. 1982–160
Presented by Interlas Welding Products Ltd

Wide-vision gas welding goggles

The *Royalette* goggles have lens ventilation ports in the frame and are used when welding, the lenses being of different colours and density according to the type of welding. The lenses in this example are tinted light green.

Inv. no. 1982–161
Presented by Interlas Welding Products

Welding goggles 1981

The two lenses are optical quality filter glass and can be changed by unscrewing the knurled ring. The main body of the goggles is soft nylon with vents top and bottom.

Inv. no. 1982–168
Presented by British American Optical Co Ltd

Welder's face mask and goggles 1982

A welder's face mask made from an aluminised fire-resistant fabric. The aluminising is deposited on both faces of a plastic film which is applied to the fabric. The light weight and heat insulation of the mask are claimed to make it particularly suitable for use in confined or hot environments. This mask was first marketed in 1982.

Inv. no. 1982–1380
Presented by Huntingdon Fusion Techniques Ltd

Plastic eyeshade

The method of keeping glare from the eyes by providing a hat or head band with a protruding peak is extremely old. This *Portia* eyeshade in a green, transparent plastic is attached to an elastic strap. It was used by the late C H Gibbs-Smith a noted aeronautical historian.

Inv. no. 1983–163
Presented by C H Gibbs-Smith.

Mallock-Armstrong ear defender plugs 1915

Examples of the first attempt at scientifically designed hearing protection, used by artillerymen during World War 1.

Inv. No. 1981–779 pt
Presented by the RAF Institute of Community Medicine

Pre-production model ear wardens 1944

Designed by the Harvard Acoustical Laboratory and regarded as a classic design of soft rubber ear plug. A wooden tapered shape was supplied for use in inserting the plugs, a small tab on the plug makes it easy to pull it out.

Inv. no. 1981–779 pt
Presented by RAF Institute of Community Medicine

'Sonex' ear defenders 1950s

Another example of the small rubber ear plug hearing protector.

Inv. no. 1981–779 pt
Presented by RAF Institute of Community Medicine

Australian Mk I ear plug

This ear plug is made from chlorobutadiene and has an oval cross-section with two flanges at the innermost end to facilitate retention and ensure a good seal. It was tested in 1954 (Report No. R5/74, Department of Clinical Medicine, RAF) and found to be moderately effective but uncomfortable and badly fitting (probably due to its availability in only one size).

Inv. no. 1981–779 pt
Presented by the RAF Institute of Community Medicine

European Vibraphone Company plugs 1958

These metal inserts of curious shape attenuated sudden loud noise. They were not widely used, possibly because, being metal, they were uncomfortable when worn for long periods.

Inv. no. 1981–779 pt
Presented by RAF Institute of Community Medicine

Noise helmet and jacket 1965

When development work began on the high power jet engines for the TSR2 aircraft it was believed that the noise levels would reach the point at which special protection would be necessary. At extremely high sound levels the vibrations will affect the skull and jaw and also the body of a person exposed to them. The lead lined helmet covers and supports the skull and jaw and the sleeveless, lead lined PVC jacket with quilted fibreglass under the inner nylon lining, damps out sound waves impinging on the body. However, tests showed that the noise levels encountered did not require this protection and the weight of jacket (15 kg) and helmet made work hot and tiring for the engineers.

Inv. no. 1983–1071
Lent by the RAF Institute of Community Medicine.

ERDEfenders 1968

Developed by the Explosive Research and Development Establishment of the former Ministry of Technology especially for their use. The cups of an ear defender have had inserted in them two microphone-amplifier-earphone assemblies. The amplifier circuits are limited so that the earphone output cannot exceed some 90dB, up to that level normal hearing operates but loud noises temporarily switch off the amplifiers and give the normal ear defender protection. This enabled workers to hear ordinary conversation and shouted orders but to be protected from explosive noise.

Inv. no. 1982–1072
Lent by the RAF Institute of Community Medicine

'Maxiguard' ear defenders 1974

An ear defender with an unusual elliptical cup shape intended to give high internal volume to the cups and so improve the low frequency performance. The head band would be worn at the back of the head instead of over the crown making it possible to wear the defenders with a safety helmet. Tests indicated that the performance was disappointing possibly due to insufficient head band tension and poor sealing round the ears.

Inv. no. 1982–1072A   Neg 272/84
Lent by the RAF Institute of Community Medicine

Lightweight ear defenders

All-plastic ear muffs which are inexpensive and effective. Foam cushions surround the ear and provide the seal.

Inv. no. 1980–1658
Presented by W Dickins & Co Ltd

Heavy-duty ear defenders

Intended for use in the noisiest conditions these *Viking* ear muffs have heavy gauge plastic shell ear covers with a strengthened spring head band and liquid-filled cushions to give a better seal.

Inv. no. 1981–1625
Presented by Bilsom International Ltd

Safety helmet with ear defenders

The need for dual protection has led to helmets designed to take a number of accessories like these *Adda-muff* units.

Inv. no. 1980–775
Presented by Safety Products Ltd

Lightweight ear defenders

The *Universal* ear defender is light (175 gms) and offers attenuation over the range of 50 to 10,000 Hz. The two ear cups contain foam and are connected by a head strap.

Inv. no. 1984–64
Presented by Martindale Protection Ltd

Target shooting ear defenders

Marksman ear muffs have the right hand shell moulded to accommodate the gunstock.

Inv. no. 1981–1626
Presented by Bilsom International Ltd

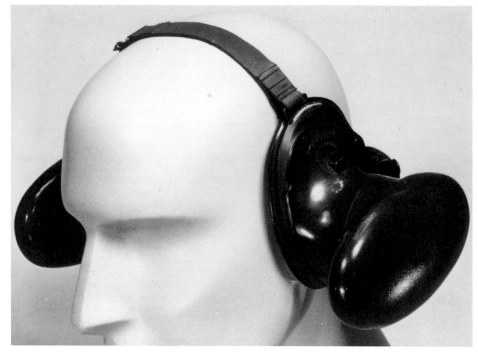

Maxiguard ear defenders 1974,
Inv no 1983–1072A

Ear plug gunfire protectors 1981

These are a contemporary version of the original *Mallock-Armstrong* design. A thin diaphragm between wire gauze in the central orifice of the plug passes speech but protects against gunfire.

Inv. no. 1983–7
Presented by Anticoustic Ltd

Ear plug gunfire protectors 1981

The *Gunfenders* earplugs include a pierced metal diaphragm to pass speech but damp out explosive noise.

Inv. no. 1981–1622
Presented by Racal Safety Ltd

Acoustic valve ear protectors 1981

These *Sonovalve* muff type protectors have a manually operated valve which closes for protection against general, continuous noise. When opened ordinary speech can be heard but explosive noise will still be damped. The acoustic valve used was developed by Racal Safety Ltd.

Inv. no. 1983–866
Presented by Racal Safety Ltd

Ear down and preformed down plugs

Simple hearing protection can be given by inserting a wadding plug into the ear. This material is wool but in the past glassfibre has also been used.

Inv. no. 1981–1623, 24
Presented by Bilsom International Ltd

Foam plastic ear plugs

In dirty conditions the ear can become infected by the action of continually remoulding ear down when the simple plug formed from it becomes loose and slips out of the ear channel. These *EAR* foam plugs can be moulded to fit the ear channel and will remain in place without coming loose. After use they can be thrown away.

Inv. no. 1981–404
Presented by Regent Dispo

Earplug gunfire protectors Inv. 1981–1622
Inv. no. 1983–7

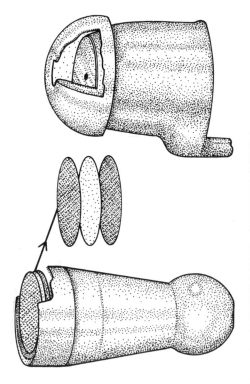

Reusable ear plugs

Comfit plugs are made from soft silicone rubber and can be sterilised in boiling water after use. A long stem makes them easy to fit and remove. There are small, medium and large pairs, the first two sizes having a separate inserter.

Inv. no. 1982–157
Presented by Totectors Ltd

Linked ear plugs

These *Caboflex* hearing protectors make a lightweight alternative to the larger ear-muff hearing protectors. The foam-filled ear pods swivel to fit each individual ear canal and can be renewed easily or washed. They are useful for workers who move in and out of noisy areas since they can be slipped out of the ears and left to hang round the neck until next needed.

Inv. no. 1982–1765
Presented by Cabot Safety Ltd

Noise dosemeter

In noisy factories it may be necessary to make a survey to discover how much noise a worker is exposed to during the day. This meter would be carried in the pocket and has a microphone which can be attached to the lapel so it is near the wearer's head. The noise picked up by the microphone is converted into a digital display, gradually adding it up so that at the end of a set period of time the amount of noise exposure can be read off.

Inv. no. 1982–166
Lent by Computer Engineering Ltd

Integrating sound level meter with octave filter

An instrument intended for general noise surveys and precision measurements. Besides the more normal measurements of noise levels the instrument contains 31 active band pass filters and a flat (all pass) mode. Noise and vibrations can thus be analysed to show the range of frequencies occuring and their relative strengths. The circuitry includes provision for connection to other instruments, including chart recorders.
This example (CEL-175, type 1) is currently in use with a demonstration showing the effect of ear defenders on high and low frequency noise.

Inv. no. 1983–1084
Lent by Computer Engineering Ltd

Vinyl rough chip finish and chain mail gloves, Inv. nos. 1980–1586, 1980–1584 (entry for latter on p. 48)

Arthritis mitts

The electrically heated, knitted gloves and underwear developed for service pilots have been adapted to 6 volt DC operation as pain relieving arthritis mitts. They are not intended as a working glove.

Inv. no. 1980–1557
Presented by Vacuum Reflex Ltd

Clean room gloves (plain and mesh styles)

In clean room areas workers use gloves like these to avoid contaminating the products they are handling. The mesh pair of gloves have polyurethane, transfer-coated palms and finger tips.

Inv. no. 1980–1567
Presented by Multifabs Ltd

Rough chip finish gloves

These plastic gloves have a rough finish of PVC chips to give extra resistance to wear when handling very abrasive materials.

Inv. no. 1980 1586 pt   Neg 198/82 with
                          Inv. no. 1980–1584 pt
Presented by Safety Specialists Ltd

Ventilation-back gloves

In hot working conditions plastic gloves can make hands very sweaty. To provide some ventilation gloves can be dipped leaving a section of the backs uncoated.

Inv. no. 1980–1586 pt
Presented by Safety Specialists Ltd

Heat resistant gloves (2 pairs)

The fabric for the gloves is *Fortamid*, a needlefelt compounded of *Nomex* fibre, flame retardant rayon and polyester scrim. It is intended as a replacement for asbestos and has low thermal conductivity and scorch characteristics. The second pair give added protection to the backs of the hands and the thumbs through the aluminising applied to the fabric.

Inv. no. 1980–1586 pt
Presented by Safety Specialists Ltd

Double dipped PVC gloves

An extra thickness of plastic on the lining achieved by a second dipping gives longer life in use.

Inv. no. 1980–1586 pt
Presented by Safety Specialists Ltd

Heavyweight, textured plastic gloves

A special dipping process is used to produce these *Karapass* gloves. Their thick palms and textured surface gives a softer feel and increase their resistance to wear.

Inv. no. 1980–1586 pt
Presented by Safety Specialists Ltd

Canadian rigger's style gloves

Made to a Canadian pattern with palms, thumbs, finger tips and knuckle protectors in leather 1.2–21.3 mm thick. The backs are heavy duty cotton with a rubberized safety cuff. There is a cotton fleece lining.

Inv. no. 1980–1586 pt
Presented by Safety Specialists Ltd

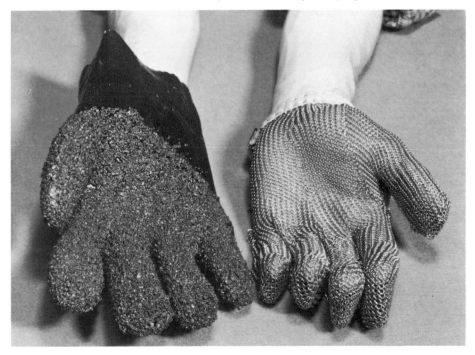

Canadian rigger's style plastic section gloves

Resembling the rigger's style leather-palmed gloves, these *Gripp-o-plast* gloves have pimpled vinyl panels on palm, thumb and fingers, to resist abrasion and improve the grip. The fabric is liquid repellant and the gloves can be machine washed several times without deterioration.

Inv. no. 1980–1586 pt
Presented by Safety Specialists Ltd

Asbestos gloves

Made of finely-woven asbestos over a cotton lining.

Inv. no. 1980–1592
Presented by Jelaco Ltd

Coated asbestos mitts

This pair has been coated with plastic to give extra resistance to abrasion and heat. These *Lasgreen* mitts also have a thick thermal lining and can be used on either hand.

Inv. no. 1980–1593
Presented by Jelaco Ltd

Coated leather gloves

These gloves are made from heavy chrome leather, plastic coated for extra resistance to abrasion and heat, with a thermal insulating lining. The thumb is reinforced to prevent the seam bursting. The gloves are reversible and can be worn on either hand giving longer economic life.

Inv. no. 1980–1594
Presented by Jelaco Ltd

Welder's lined leather gloves

Inv. no. 1980–1595
Presented by Ensum (London) Ltd

Armoured hand pad

The practice of reinforcing leather with added rivets or studs is very old. This hand pad is in chrome leather with a double palm and would be used in handling very hard and rough materials such as bricks, sheet metal, or castings.

Inv. no. 1980–1655
Presented by W Dickins & Co Ltd

Shotblaster's gloves

Elbow length made from heavy gauge rubber. Dimpled palms and fingers give better grip and also resist wear longer.

Inv. no. 1980–1656
Presented by W Dickins & Co Ltd

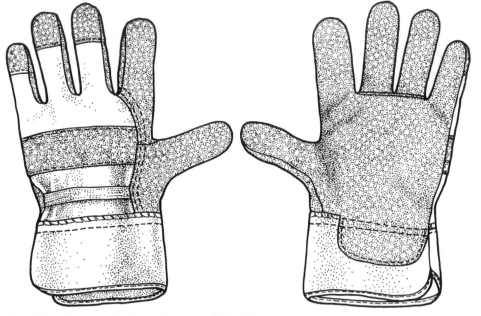

Canadian riggers style gloves, Inv. no. 1980–1586pt

Vinyl impregnated cotton gloves

These *Tuff Duck* gloves are made to a Canadian pattern from vinyl impregnated cotton fabric. They are not a dipped plastic glove but sewn.

Inv. no. 1980–1657
Presented by W Dickins & Co Ltd

Unlined rubber gloves

Lightweight, unlined rubber gloves, used where flexibility and sensitivity of touch are of paramount importance.

Inv. no. 1980–1800
Presented by Bristol Oilskin & Overall Company Ltd

Cold store gloves

The gloves are made from good quality leather with a fleecy lining and are intended for cold store workers.

Inv. no. 1980–1801
Presented by Bristol Oilskin & Overall Company Ltd

Heat resistant gloves

Made from an *Aramid* fibre with a flame retardant rayon inner layer, these *Northgard* gloves are used for handling items direct from hot ovens, for welding and burning, or vulcanising processes. A hot metal bar at 200°C will not char the gloves and it could be held for 32 seconds. Molten metal at 327°C will not penetrate the surface. With such good thermal insulation the gloves can also be used for working with very low temperature liquid gases.

Inv. no. 1981–18
Presented by James North & Sons Ltd

Loop pile fabric gloves

Northerm gloves are made from a heavyweight cotton yarn knitted into a loop pile. The loops trap air and so provide insulation against heat or cold as well as giving a firm grip even when oil-soaked. The gloves are reversible, and can be worn on either hand giving a longer economic life.

Inv. no. 1981–19
Presented by James North & Sons Ltd

Disposable medical gloves

These PVC gloves fill the need for a cheap disposable glove to use in simple examination of patients and prevent cross-infection.

Inv. no. 1981–402
Presented by Regent Dispo

Surgeon's gloves

The *Marigold* surgical gloves are made from natural rubber which is preferred by many surgeons because of the greater flexibility and sensitivity it gives.

Inv. no. 1981–403
Presented by Regent Dispo

Industrial gauntlet gloves

These gauntlets illustrate some of the designs for general industrial hand protection once produced by the donors:
1. Chrome leather with soft gussetted cuff. (pair)
2. Chrome leather with double leather layer on the thumb and index finger. (single)
3. Cotton and canvas with chrome leather palm and finger; fleecy lined. This type has a very flexible canvas cuff. (single)

Inv. no. (1) 1981–695 (2) 1981–696 (3) 1981–697
Presented by Gloverall Ltd

Glass handling gauntlets

These latex gauntlets have a reinforced palm and non-slip fingers for handling sheet glass safely.

Inv. no. 1981–707
Presented by Ensum (London) Ltd

Electrically heated gloves 1950s

Inner gloves of this type were worn by Canberra bomber crewmen. The resistance wire then available for heating circuits was not very flexible and had to be applied to the outside of the glove; this was often done in zig-zag fashion.

Inv. no. 1981–880

Hand hat

In the past a glass worker seeking to protect his hand when lifting a hot article would snatch off his hat and wrap it over his fingers and thumb. From this custom comes the hand hat, a fingerless, thumbless mitten in heavy wool felt.

Inv. no. 1981–1505   Neg 258/84
Presented by Pilkington Brothers PLC

Nylon latex-coated gloves

These heavy nylon *criss-cross*, knitted gloves have been given a coating of latex in lattice form to improve their grip and resistance to abrasion. PVC can also be coated onto gloves in this manner.

Inv. no. 1981–1718
Presented by Comasec Safety Ltd

Disposable vinyl gloves

These seamless, liquid proof, disposable gloves are powdered inside to provide a close fit and sensitivity of touch for delicate assembly work.

Inc. no. 1981–1929
Presented by Contamination Control Apparel Ltd

Cold weather working mitts in a machine knitted fabric

These three Norwegian designs of working mitts are intended for outdoor use in very cold weather.
1. 'Work' mitts with palm and thumb slits in knitted polyamid with a fleecy lining in the same materials.
2. 'Grip' mitts in knitted polyamid with vinyl dots on the palm and thumb to improve the grip.
3. 'Carpenter' mitt in knitted polyamid with palm and thumb slits, vinyl dots to improve grip and *Velcro* strips on the backs to hold the palm open.

Inv. no. 1982–440
Presented by Helly-Hansen (UK) Ltd

Weedkilling glove

The *Croptex* glove was originally developed for use in the tropics where spraying cactus with weedkiller was ineffective as the spray evaporated before penetrating the surface of the plants. Closing the hand once or twice to compress the rubber bulb in the glove palm forces air down a tube into the weedkiller tank (carried on a belt) and thus drive the liquid up another tube and over a sponge also in the palm. The plastic covering sponge and bulb has minute perforations in it allowing the weedkiller to seep out. By sweeping the hand over the cactus or gripping the weed a coating of liquid is applied.

Inv. no. 1983–1085
Lent by James North & Sons Ltd

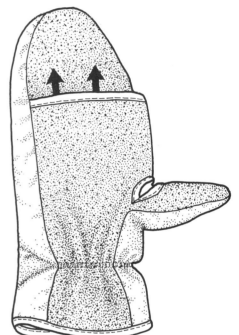

Norwegian cold weather working mitt (*Carpenter*), inv. no. 1982–440

Glass worker's hand hat, Inv no 1981–1505

Abrasion resistant gloves

In *Hycron* gloves nitrile butadiene rubber is the impregnating agent and gives a high degree of resistance to abrasion. The jersey lining has been made with curved pre-flexed fingers and a 'wing' thumb to give greater comfort when working. The glove is also machine washable.

Inv. no. 1982–1809
Presented by Edmont Europe

Cut and abrasion resistant gloves

These *Hynit* gloves are impregnated with nitrile butadiene rubber and resist cuts and abrasions.

Inv. no. 1982–1810
Presented by Edmont Europe

Abrasion resistant glove with safety cuff

Hyd-Tuf gloves have been developed as an alternative to leather palm gloves and have been designed to give good manual dexterity and sensitivity. The coating material is nitrile butadiene rubber. The gloves outwear certain types of leather palm gloves by five times and, being more flexible, are easier and safer and more comfortable for the worker.

Inv. no. 1982–1811
Presented by Edmont Europe

Heat and cut resistant gloves

These *Polysafe* knitted gloves have an outer terrycloth finish in *Kevlar* yarn and an inner lining of cotton. The normal maximum handling temperature is 200°C and they will give protection from accidental contact at 250–300°C.

Inv. no. 1983–168
Presented by Bennett Safetywear Ltd

Heavy-duty canvas and rubber glove

This glove was found on a London building site and very little is known about its construction and use. It appears to be suitable for heavy work, such as handling bricks, pipes and the like.

It consits of a fold of heavy-duty canvas (extending over the wrist). Attached to this, by means of three studs, is a sheet of (3mm) rubber, which covers the hand area only.

It is quite well made, and is possibly a 'one-off' item.

Inv. no. 1984–188
Presented by the Worshipful Company of Glovers

Industrial gauntlets

A design which was produced for the Ministry of Defence for arctic warfare. The glove portion of the gauntlet is made of soft leather and it has a man-made fibre wrist protector. There are four press studs around the rim for attaching the gauntlet to the sleeve. On the back of each gauntlet is a wool pad for wiping perspiration off the brow or cleaning a visor or goggles.

Inv. no. 1984–189
Presented by the Worshipful Company of Glovers

PVC cuff protectors

The custom of wearing oversleeves of cotton or linen to protect the clothes of clerks, storemen and the like was common in the 19th century. Some nurses' uniforms still include ruffled white cotton bands on the edges of their short sleeves indicative of the protectors which would have covered and secured rolled up sleeves. These examples, about 2 inches deep, are made from transparent PVC.

Inv. no. 1981–698
Presented by Gloverall Ltd

'Goodyear' welted shoes with protective steel toe cap

Made by traditional methods, this type of leather boot and shoe, although expensive in terms of labour and materials, gives very long wear. The soles can be repaired many times and the boot will retain its shape. One shoe has been sectioned to show construction with protective steel toe cap.

Inv. no. 1982–150   Neg 1342/82
Presented by Totectors Ltd

Direct vulcanised boots with protective steel toe cap

After the upper parts have been made and attached to the insole, the boot is clamped into a mould. The mould contains pieces of pre-heated rubber compound and the bottom section can be forced upward with a pressure of 6–800 lbs per square inch. The pressure and heat cause the rubber to flow and the sulphur already in the compound vulcanises it to give a hard sole. Because of the heat only chrome tanned leathers can be used for the uppers. Resistance to oil is produced by adding nitrile to the rubber compound. One boot has been sectioned to show construction.

Inv. no. 1982–151   Neg as above
Presented by Totectors Ltd

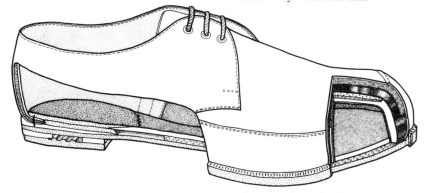

Construction of a 'goodyear' welted shoe, inv. no. 1981–150

Construction of a vulcanised boot, inv. no. 1981–151

Injection moulded shoe with protective steel toe cap and sectioned boot

The completed upper and insole are clamped into a mould and molten PVC is injected through a connection in the side of the mould. When the mould is full, the PVC flow is automatically cut off and the new sole allowed to cool. By refrigerating the mould this cooling time can be cut to 2½ minutes. Introduced in 1963, this process has largely replaced direct vulcanising. A 'Chelsea' style boot has been sectioned to show construction.

Inv. no. 1982–152　　　Neg as above
Presented by Totectors Ltd

Injection moulded PU 'trainers' with protective steel toe cap

The injection moulding process was developed in the late 1960s. Resin and pre-polymer held in storage tanks are fed by gravity through heated hoses to a mixing machine which injects the compound into the mould carrying the upper parts of the shoe. The two liquids react in the mould to form polyurethane; the gas produced by the reaction gives the sole a microcellular structure. These examples are in the popular style of the leisure and sports shoes known as trainers; one has been sectioned.

Inv. no. 1982–153　　　Neg as above
Presented by Totectors Ltd

Construction of an injection moulded shoe, inv. no. 1981–152

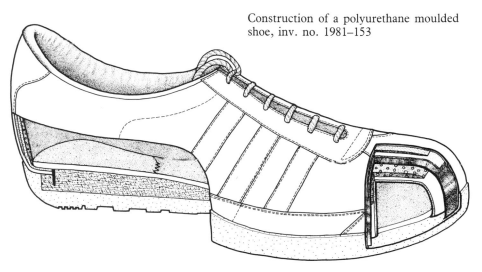

Construction of a polyurethane moulded shoe, inv. no. 1981–153

Safety toecaps and inner sole plate

These are typical of the type of protection devices inserted into boots and shoes during the manufacturing process.

Inv. no. 1982–154　　　Neg as above
Presented by Totectors Ltd

Child's canoe boots and snow shoes c. 1900

The leather canoe boots are of a type worn by early traders and woodsmen in Canada, developed from North American Indian footwear. The boot protects the foot but is flexible enough to be used with snow shoes.

The snow shoes were made for walking on deep loose snow. They are no longer made and rarely used by the Indians, these examples came from the Alongquian-speaking tribe in Eastern Canada.

Inv. no. 1983–126 & 127
Purchased

Logger's boots 1920–1940

These are typical of the leather boots used by Canadian loggers in the years before the Second World War. The metal nails – known as corks – give a good grip on the

surface of wet logs. The boots are heavily greased to make them waterproof.

Inv. no. 1983–238
Purchased

Hobnailed boots and leather gaiters

Typical countryman's boots from South Yorkshire of a pattern that was widely worn during the nineteenth and first half of the twentieth century. The nails prolonged the life of the leather sole.

Inv. no. 1980–1481, 1482
Presented by Mr & Mrs A Teasdale

Chemical worker's clogs c. 1930–50

Leather soled boots would quickly be damaged by acid or alkali spillages on the floors of chemical plants and so the wooden soled clog has been used for many years. The wooden sole also provides insulation against heat or cold. This pair with wood soles and leather uppers has clog irons fitted to the sole to improve the wearing qualities.

Inv. no. 1980–1190
Presented by ICI Organic Chemical Works

Foundry clogs

The wooden-soled clog has been widely used in many industries because of its hard wearing qualities and resistance to both heat and cold and also to damp underfoot conditions. To guard against metal splashes and hot cinders or slag lodging in the fastening foundry clogs like these examples have an apron fronted upper and quick release fastenings.

Inv. no. 1980–1589
Presented by Jelaco Ltd

Foundry boots and gaiters

The development of synthetic rubbers which are suitable for use in arduous foundry conditions has led to the gradual replacement of the wooden-soled moulder's boots. Gaiters in leather, neoprene or nitrile rubber are worn to give added protection against metal splash. These examples are typical of contemporary foundry wear.

Inv. no. 1980–1654
Presented by W. Dickins & Co Ltd

High-leg foundry boots

The non-ferrous metal foundries appear to have been the first to use this style of boot. The trousers must be worn with bottoms over the boot to prevent hot particles lodging in the boot top. These examples have a heat and oil resistant sole to BS 4676 200 Joules.

Inv. no. 1981–2031
Presented by Goliath Footwear CWS Ltd

Experimental insulated boots

Glass furnacemen have, from time to time, to work on the crown of the furnace and, even using thick-soled wooden clogs, their feet get uncomfortably hot. The Protective Clothing Department of Messrs. Pilkingon Bros. produced these clogs as an answer to this problem. The normal wooden clog sole has been given a thick inner cushion of insulation and the upper part fitted with a metallised, padded covering. Subsequently the steel toecap was added.

Although the boots were very effective it has not been possible to bring them into use because of the difficulty of finding a manufacturer to make the small number of pairs required.

Inv. no. 1983–682   Neg 1101/82/9
                  with Inv. no. 1982–1770
                                  1707/81
Lent by Pilkington Brothers PLC   233/84

US Army extreme cold weather rubber boots 1981

Specially designed for arctic conditions the boots have a double layer of insulation separated by an air space in the uppers.

When the wearer boards an aircraft a small valve on the side of the uppers is opened to equalize the air pressure inside the boot, which would otherwise balloon as the plane ascended.

Inv. no. 1981–1020   Neg 1105/82/6
Presented by the Bata Shoe Corporation of Canada

Glassworkers' boots 1981

The boots have *Kevlar* inserts included in their uppers to give protection against piercing by broken glass. The sole is vulcanised rubber with very high oil resistance properties and incorporates the usual protective steel midsole plate and toe cap.

Inv. no. 1981–2029
Presented by Goliath Footwear CWS Ltd

Forestry worker's boots 1981

Forestry workers who regularly use chain saws need special protection for their feet and legs. These boots have a *Kevlar* lining included in the lower parts and a

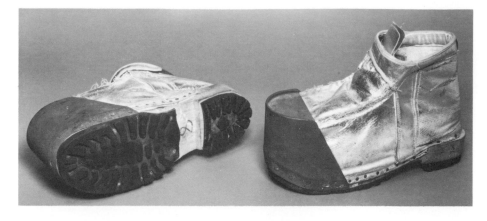

Experimental insulated boots for glass furnacemen, Inv no 1983–682

US Army extreme cold weather boots, Inv no 1981–1020 (below)

JOHN FREEMAN

Construction of a glass worker's boot, inv. no. 1981–2029

protective ballistic nylon shin guard for the leg. The leather is water repellant and the vulcanised rubber soles are heat and oil resistant. The design has been approved by the Forestry Commission and the steel toecap conforms to DIN 4843.

Inv. no. 1981–2030
Presented by Goliath Footwear CWS Ltd

Unlined wellingtons with slip-resistant soles

Nora Oilmax wellingtons are resistant to

oils, fats, salts, mild fertilisers, most acids and alkalis. Since they are unlined they can be washed out and the slip-resistant soles give an extra safety factor during wear.

Inv. no. 1980–1799
Presented by the Bristol Oilskin and Overall Co Ltd

Wading boots

The *Streamfisher* thigh high rubber boots have a fabric backed sponge insole and a cleated sole of crepe rubber incorporating cork granules which gives added grip on watercovered surfaces.

Inv. no. 1981–667
Lent by Uniroyal Ltd

Women's cannery rubber boots

These examples have non-slip soles and moulded, vulcanised, protective toecaps. As is common with this style the boots have a smooth lining to permit them to be hosed out.

Inv. no. 1981–668
Lent by Uniroyal Ltd

Fireman's rubber boots

Produced to meet an exacting Home Office specification (No. A17) these boots incorporate pull-on loops, protective toecaps and midsole reinforcement over the insteps, flame resistant out-soles, and padded shins and ankles. The sole is designed to give a secure footing on ladders.

Inv. no. 1981–669
Lent by Uniroyal Ltd

Antistatic half knee boots

Additives in the rubber compound, used to make these boots, ensures that any static electrical charge generated by the wearer's clothes will leak harmlessly to earth. The boots meet the requirements of BS 5451E.

Inv. no. 1981–1336
Presented by BTR Silvertown Ltd

Fishing boots

The *Seafarer* rubber boots are three-quarter length with deep-cleated soles and heels and sponge inner soles. The top of the boot can be laced up.

Inv. no. 1981–1337
Presented by BTR Silvertown Ltd

General protection rubber boots

The boots have internal steel toecaps and full length spring steel mid-soles. *Armasol* boots give good general protection when worn, for example, on building sites. They conform to BS1870 part 2.

Inv. no. 1981–1338
Presented by BTR Silvertown Ltd

Digging rubber boots

Trenchers boots are fitted with non-metallic, safety digging pads and with added reinforcement on the inner side of the legs. They conform to BS1870 part 2.

Inv. no. 1981–1339
Presented by BTR Silvertown Ltd

Insulated rubber boots

Bullseye boots are tested up to 10,000 volts and have resinated toecaps for extra protection.

Inv. no. 1981–1340
Presented by BTR Silvertown Ltd

Antistatic rubber boots

Compounded so that the insoles and outsoles are electrically conducting, these boots would be worn where there is a risk of explosion being caused by a spark. They have internal steel toecaps, and they conform to BS3825.

Inv. no. 1981–1341
Presented by BTR Silvertown Ltd

Rubber/PVC boots 1982

A design introduced in 1982 made from nitrile rubber and PVC compound. There are carbon steel protective toecaps and mid-soles with a suction-grip pattern and easy-to-clean nylon linings. The *Safety Plus* boots meet BS 1870 pt 3.

Inv. no. 1983–1355
Presented by Dunlop Industrial and Protective Footwear

Rubber/PVC boots 1982

Made from a nitrile rubber/PVC compound the *Warwick* industrial boots are meant for heavy duty use and are to BS 6159. The boots have kick-off spurs moulded onto the back of the heels.

Inv. no. 1983–1356
Presented by Dunlop Industrial & Protective Footwear

Rubber/PVC boots 1982

Similar to Inv. nos. 1983–1355 & 1356, the *Metasol* boots are fitted with corrosion resistant steel midsoles to BS 6159.

Inv. no. 1983–1357
Presented by Dunlop Industrial and Protective Footwear

Protective toecapped boots with stubguard

Workers handling packing cases or regularly kneeling to work often wear away the toes of their boots so that the metal protective cap shows through. This can be dangerous as well as unsightly so these *Keysafe* boots have an added thickness of rubber at the edge of the soles to take the wear and prevent the abrasion of the toecaps.

Inv. no. 1983–370
Presented by Rely Upon Protection

Clean room overboots and overshoes

Knee length overboots and overshoes made from ceramic terylene with hard-wearing rubber soles.

Inv. no. 1981–1927
Presented by Contamination Control Apparel Ltd

Antistatic, disposable overshoes

Overshoes, made from *Tyvek*, with a carbon-loaded PVC strip attached to the soles and looped inside so it makes contact with the wearer's outdoor shoe. The carbon-loaded strip conducts electricity and so ensures any static electric charge leaks harmlessly to earth.

Inv. no. 1981–1228
Presented by Contamination Control Apparel Ltd

Ballet shoes 1982

Ballerina's shoes have a special toe cap to enable the dancer to go 'on point' without damaging the toes. After a single performance blocked shoes can be so badly worn they have to be discarded. Dancers will often darn the fabric at the toe of new shoes to increase their useful life. There are two pairs with one shoe sectioned to show how they are built up.

Inv. no. 1982–1770   Neg 1101/82/9
                         with Inv. no. 1983–682
Presented by the Royal Ballet

Smith's leather apron

The toughness and high retained water content of leather have made it a favourite material for protection. This smith's apron is split at the front to allow him to grasp a horse's leg between his knees when shoeing.

Inv. no. 1980–1585
Presented by W Dickins & Co Ltd

Nitrile rubber apron

This synthetic rubber is very resistant to animal fats and greases found in abattoirs and tanneries.

Inv. no. 1980–1802
Presented by Bristol Oilskin & Overall Co Ltd

Chrome leather apron

Very hard wearing, this kind of apron would be used by workers doing grinding, or handling rough and abrasive materials, or welding.

Inv. no. 1980–1803
Presented by Bristol Oilskin & Overall Co Ltd

Moleskin brewery apron

This hardwearing cotton fabric is traditionally used for draymen's aprons.

Inv. no. 1980–1804
Presented by Bristol Oilskin & Overall Co Ltd

Lightweight coated nylon apron

Intended for female workers this *Northylon* apron is coated with PVC and would be used in such industries as food canning.

Inv. no. 1981–16
Presented by James North & Sons Ltd

Medium weight PVC apron

This is intended for use when there is a danger of coming into prolonged contact with mineral oils which will cause skin disease.

Inv. no. 1981–17
Presented by James North & Sons Ltd

Butcher's apron 1981

A polyurethane-coated nylon apron in the traditional blue and white stripes for use in butcher's shops.

Inv. no. 1981–384
Presented by MG Rubber Company Ltd

Heavyweight rubber apron

Used where the wearer requires protection from acids and alkalis.

Inv. no. 1981–385
Presented by M G Rubber Company Ltd

Proofed cotton canvas apron

Gives good wear and repels liquids.

Inv. no. 1981–592
Presented by Bristol Oilskin & Overall Co Ltd.

Glass cutter's apron

Used in the flat glass industry where protection against cuts is needed. The apron has a wire mesh insert and a felt patch at bench level.

Inv. no. 1981–1507
Presented by Pilkington Brothers PLC

Beaverteen apron

Worn by *Triplex* glass polishers to soak up splashes of the paraffin used as a lubricant.

Inv. no. 1981–1508
Presented by Pilkington Brothers PLC

Butcher's apron, 1964
Cotton-backed rubber

Inv. no. 1982–974
Presented by K McWilton

Glass handler's jacket and leggings, 1950s

Up to about 1955, thick layers of clothing were worn by glass handlers. To supply a lighter yet more protective garment Pilkington Brothers Protective Clothing Department designed and made this style of jacket and leggings. Wire mesh set into the sleeves and shoulders affords protection; the sleeves are perforated for ventilation. The leg shields have the same wire mesh inserts and are reinforced vertically with flexible, plastic-coated, steel strips. The foot cover includes a 22 gauge aluminium cap sewn in together with a felt pad.

Inv. no. 1981–1506
Presented by Pilkington Brothers PLC

Welder's jacket 1980

Like the blacksmith the welder needs protection from the sparks and metal spatter created by his work. Leather jackets like this example give the best protection and are often worn with leggings or an apron to protect the lower half of the body.

Inv. no. 1980–1653
Presented by W Dickins & Co Ltd

Fluorescent safety waistcoat

The waistcoat made in bright orange PVC is intended to show up the wearer in poor visibility and includes *Scotchlite* panels to reflect light from vehicle headlamps. The choice of colour for such clothes has varied over the years, orange, red and lime green are currently available. A new colour, saturn yellow, began to come into use in the early 1980s as it gives better visibility under sodium street lighting.

Inv. no. 1981–411
Presented by Arthur Millar Ltd

Mail glove and apron

In large abattoirs and wholesale butchery departments there is always a danger of serious injury when the men are working at speed. Chain mail gloves, protective armlets, and aprons give protection from cuts and stab wounds. Made in stainless steel to avoid corrosion, with each link individually welded, these items can readily be sterilised after use. This glove has a wrist guard; normal practice is to wear one only on the left hand as this would be the hand at risk from the knife held in the right hand.
    The gloves and aprons are also used by workers handling sharp-edged materials such as steel plates and the aprons will be worn by chemical accident teams when moving potentially explosive chemicals in glass bottles or jars.

Inv. no. 1983–1070
Lent by British Rawhide Belting Co Ltd

Chain mail glove, armlet and aluminium apron 1980

The apron is made from a series of small interlinked aluminium segments and is lighter in weight than the stainless steel mail apron (Inv. no. 1983–1070). In abattoirs a fabric apron must be worn over the top as the linked segments quickly pick up fragments of meat as the carcases are handled.

Inv. no. 1980–1584
                Neg 198/82 mail glove with
Purchased   Inv. no. 1980–1586 pt

Steel armoured waistcoat, early 1940s

This waistcoat was to be worn under a uniform jacket. The ballistic protection is given by two layers of small steel plates, each one enclosed in a separate pocket. The waistcoat weighs 10 kg.

Inv. no. 1983–1079
Lent by SCRDE, Ministry of Defence

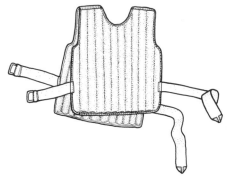

Armoured waistcoat from World War II, inv. no. 1983–1079

Undershirt armour 1982 and flexible armour test pack

This undershirt armour is meant for use by politicians or other public figures likely to be at risk from ballistic attack. Weight of the armour is 1.6 kg. Ceramic armour insert plates can be added to protect against high velocity rifle fire and a detachable panel provides protection for the abdomen.
    The test pack shows the resistance of *Kevlar* fabric armour; the 9mm bullets were fired at high velocity from a short range.

Inv. no. 1983–1081, 1082
Lent by Bristol Composite Materials Engineering Ltd, Avonmouth

Foresters' leg guard 1982

Leg guards made from four layers of *Kevlar* have now been introduced. These give the same degree of protection as ballistic nylon guards but are lighter and less bulky. This example has been sectioned.

Inv. no. 1982–665
Presented by W C Willis & Co Ltd

Glass worker's shin protectors

In the early years of this century little protective clothing was provided for sheet glass workers in the handling areas of the factories who simply accepted cuts as a normal hazard of working life. Some devised their own crude protection like these two examples of metal shin and foot guards.

Inv. no. 1983–683   Neg 249/84
Lent by Pilkington Brothers PLC

Neoprene foundry spats

Spat leggings are often worn as additional protection for the lower legs and insteps of foundrymen, particularly those working in casting shops where molten metal is poured from crucibles into the moulds. These examples are in neoprene but spats are also made in leather.

Inv. no. 1980–1590
Presented by Jelaco Ltd

Heavy duty industrial life jacket

The *Lifemaster* life jacket (type 3) is manufactured to BS 3595 and has 20 lbs of inherent buoyancy in the deflated state. It can be inflated by mouth to not less than 40 lbs total buoyancy.

Inv. no. 1980–1559
Presented by Vacuum Reflex Ltd

Glass worker's improvised leg shields,
Inv no 1983–683

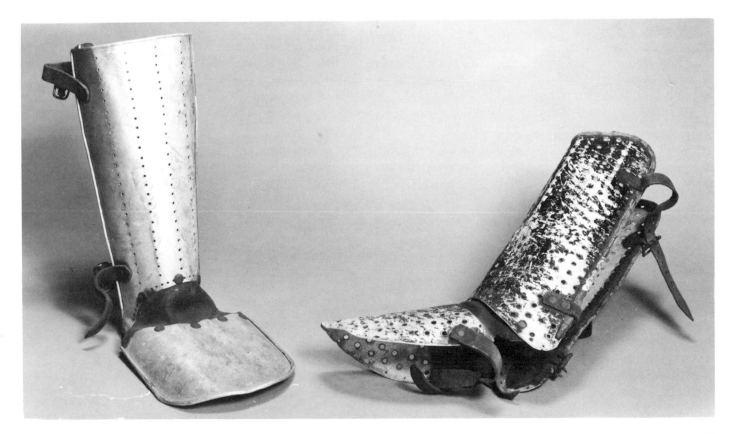

Filter masks and breathing apparatus

Pliny's reference, already noted in the introduction to this catalogue, seems to be the first mention of an industrial filter mask. During the last century workers in the chemical industries faced with noxious fumes and dust simply wrapped scarves or strips of cloth round their faces as primitive filters. Early diving apparatus which incorporated a tube delivering air to a helmet enclosing the head was the forerunner of a number of nineteenth century designs for use in atmospheres heavily polluted by smoke. Such tube-to-helmet apparatus is still specified for fire-fighting in enclosed areas on board ship. Although a number of inventions of filter masks to purify air were made during the nineteenth century they do not seem to have come into general use and during the early poison-gas attacks in the 1914–18 war only the most primitive of masks were made available. Later more efficient gas masks were devised and improvements have continued to be made. Most recent is the positive pressure face mask in which the air pressure inside the mask is higher than that of the surrounding atmosphere, to ensure leakage is only from the mask outwards.

In areas where there is insufficient oxygen present to support life then breathing apparatus has to be used. Aristotle mentions divers supplied with air from some form of container but the first diving apparatus with its own self-contained air supply was invented by W H James in 1825. The first really practical air breathing apparatus was designed by H A Fleuss in 1878 and was used in mine rescue work at the disasters at Seaham and Killingworth in 1880 and 1882. Little interest was shown in the apparatus however and not until after 1902 was further development carried out on self-contained breathing apparatus.

The marketing of new types of smoke filter masks (intended for escape purposes) in the early 1980s led to controversy. A government working party in November 1982 asked the British Standards Institution to draw up a new British Standard and guidelines for the use of the new masks. A draft standard was expected to be issued very early in 1984.

Face masks and breathing apparatus are irksome to wear for lengthy periods and in low pollution conditions other, simpler protection may be worn. In the last twenty years a number of filter masks have been introduced based on moulded fibrous material shapes fitting over the nose and mouth only which are cheap enough to throw away after use.

Smoke helmet *c.* 1900*

The *Spirelmo* helmet was produced by the Siebe Gorman Company at the beginning of this century and is a descendant of the much earlier tube-to-helmet diving apparatus. Intended for use in smoky, polluted atmospheres, the wearer is supplied with fresh air from foot bellows pumping the air into a long tube attached through a Y connection to two inlets either side of the helmet. Maximum safe distance for use would be not more than 120 feet (36m).

The helmet's crown is metal with a centrally placed valve to release excess and used air. A stiff leather face piece has two rectangular, metal framed mica windows which are hinged and can be opened or latched shut as required. A more flexible leather is used to complete the rest of the helmet and it extends down over the neck. A leather strap closes the 'skirt' against the neck.

Inv. no. 1979–392   Neg 1297/79
Purchased

Cloth smoke helmet *c.* 1910*

The *EEDS* smoke helmet consists of a cloth hood which covers the head and neck. It has a mica window held in place by a metal and canvas surround. A patent (No. 14232) was granted for the helmet in 1903 to Frederick Evans Jackson of Manchester and a portion of the specification reads:
'. . . for enabling a person to escape suffocation from smoke on the outbreak of fire by enclosing the mouth and nostrils in an envelope containing a sufficient supply of the ordinary atmosphere to breathe while descending stairs or seeking other exits from a building.'

When used the fabric would be wetted before putting on the helmet. This example was manufactured by Eeds and Co., Chorlton-cum-Hardy, Manchester and belonged to Surgeon Captain R H Knapp, RN. The original descriptive card is preserved with the helmet.

Wellcome no. A652313
Lent by the Wellcome Museum of the History of Medicine

Bellows smoke set

A fresh-air breathing apparatus very similar in principle to the earlier *Spirelmo* set (Inv. no. 1979–392). It was designed primarily to comply with Board of Trade requirements for use on board ship and is used in situations where noxious gases are present or the oxygen content of the air is low. Its design permits the wearer to breathe even if the foot bellows are not being operated. The inner half-face mask reduces carbon dioxide build up and prevents the visor misting.

Inv. no. 1983–1352
Lent by Chubb Panorama Ltd

Barton's respirator *c.* 1890*

This respirator, patented by Samuel Barton in 1872, enabled the wearer to breathe in smoky and polluted atmospheres such as those encountered after a fire. At the front of the mask is a filter of granulated charcoal layers alternating with cotton wool soaked in glycerine. An air-tight fit to the wearer's face is provided by means of a water-filled tube fixed to the inside of the mask.

Inv. no. 1930–907   Neg 179/84
Presented by the Duke of Devonshire

Bellows supplied smoke helmet, the *Spirelmo* c1900, Inv no 1979–392

Barton's respirator c1890, Inv no 1930–907

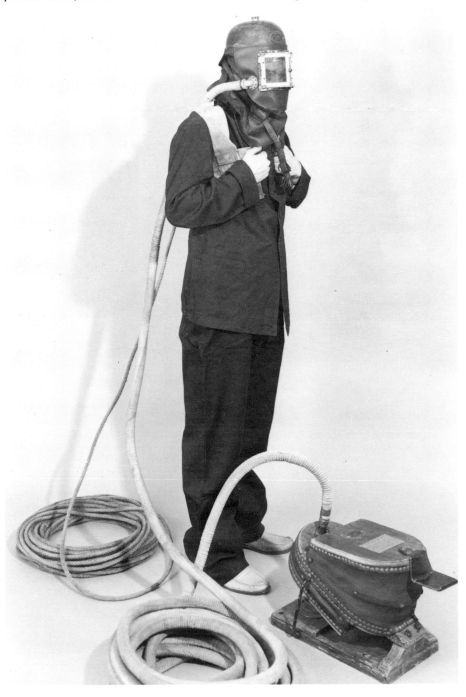

Civilian duty respirator, type C6, 1936

Introduced in 1934, the C6 duty respirator has a moulded rubber face piece, two eyepieces and a spear exhale valve. The filter canister is the same as for the C1 (Inv. no. 1982–51) but is attached to the mask by a steel clip. The respirator is carried in a canvas haversack containing an anti-dim canister.

Inv. no. 1981–786
Presented by Mr G Hearse

General civilian respirator, type C1 c. 1939

40 million of these respirators were produced between 1936 and 1939, at a cost equivalent to 12½p each. The filter is held in place simply by a rubber band, and the respirator is packed in a cardboard box or a tin canister. All civilians, including older children, were issued with these respirators during the Second World War.

Inv. no. 1982–51
Presented by Mr & Mrs D J Griffiths

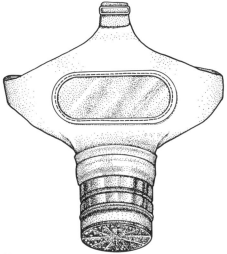

Childs respirator, Inv. no. 1981–1454

Civilian respirator, Inv. no. 1982–51
52

General service respirator MkV, c. 1941

The rubber face mask is covered in stockinette and the filter canister, which is carried in a haversack, is fitted with a long hose enabling it to be worn on the back when in use.

Inv. no. 1981–1320
Presented by the Ministry of Defence

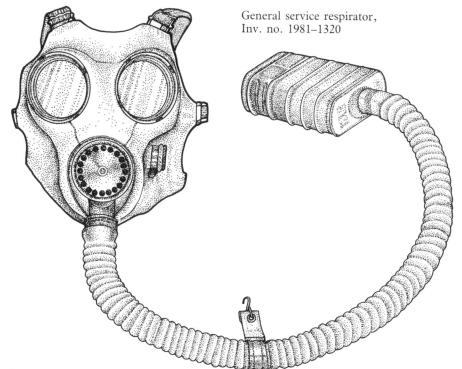

Small child's respirator, type C2 c. 1945

This respirator was made for children aged between 18 months and 4 years. It was known as the 'Mickey Mouse', in the hope that children would be less frightened by the strange appearance if it bore a popular name. The loose flap above the filter is an exhale valve.

Inv. no. 1981–1454
Presented by Miss S J Cackett

General civilian respirator, type C7 c. 1945

To ensure a good fit this respirator is made in 5 sizes, and has an air-filled cushion around the inner rim of the mask.

Inv. no. 1981–787
Presented by Mr G Hearse

General service respirator, MkVI c. 1950

This type of respirator was introduced in 1943 and has a black rubber face-piece with a side inlet for a screw-in (2½ inch thread) round canister. The exhale valve has an integral speech diaphragm. It is carried in a waterproof canvas case.

Inv. no. 1981–1321
Presented by the Ministry of Defence

General service respirator MkV, c.1941

In this example the face mask is plain rubber and the canister has a short hose for chest wear.

Inv. no. 1981–1319
Presented by the Ministry of Defence

General service respirator, Inv. no. 1981–1320

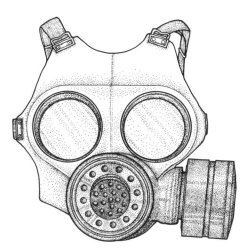

General service respirator, Inv. no. 1981–1322

General service respirator, MkVII c. 1955

The filter is mounted on the face mask so that the fighting soldier is not impeded by a hose or separate canister.

Inv. no. 1981–1322
Presented by the Ministry of Defence

Dust respirator

This simple respirator provides protection against non-toxic dust and paint spray mist. The filters can be replaced when necessary. A cotton ringlet (which can be removed for washing) ensures a close fit to the wearer's face.

Inv. no. 1981–593
Presented by Safety Products Ltd

Twin-filter dust respirator c. 1960

Respirators similar to this were used in ICI chemical plants during the 1960s. They were also used in gypsum works in Czechoslovakia during the same period.

Inv. no. 1981–1521　　Neg 1100/82/4,
196/82 with Inv. nos.
1980–771, 1981–468, 1982–421
Presented by G Hetherington Esq

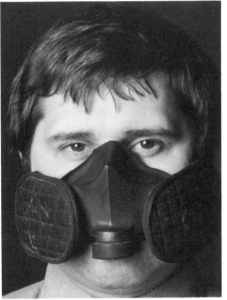

JOHN FREEMAN

Twin-filter dust respirator c1960,
Inv no 1981–1521

Powered respirator, mask and blouse

The belt-mounted respirator is powered by a battery and can supply up to 18 litres of filtered air per minute. It can be attached to:

1　A full face mask. This mask gives high efficiency protection. A 'positive pressure' inside the mask prevents unfiltered air from leaking in. The mask is made of soft pliable rubber, with upturned edges to ensure a close fit on the face. Exhaled air is vented direct into the atmosphere through a valve which also acts as a speech diaphragm.
2　A pressure ventilated blouse. This blouse, which covers the wearer from head to waist, was developed for use in atomic energy research and the pharmaceutical industry. It provides protection against airborne toxic dust particles contaminating the work area. Air is supplied to the blouse, via a pipe at the top of the transparent hood, and

it escapes through the wrists and waistband, thus providing the wearer with an air-conditioned environment. Material – *Wavelock*, a polyvinyl material impregnated with nylon.

Inv. no. 1981–459, 1981–462, 1981–461
Presented by Martindale Protection Ltd

Belt-mounted powered respirator

The *Powermask Mk III* belt-mounted respirator is powered by a rechargeable battery unit and can supply up to 120 litres of filtered air per minute. The air is fed through a hose connection to the full suit, similar to Inv. no. 1980–1416.

Alternatively a half mask, a PVC blouse, similar to Inv. no. 1981–1461, a full suit, or a full-face mask can be used with the filter unit. The circular filter case includes a pre-filter as well as the main filter. By changing the pre-filter each time the battery is charged the life of the main filter is extended. The unit is intended to provide positive pressure protection against low concentrations of organic vapours and dusts such as those encountered when spraying crops.

Inv. no. 1981–401
Lent by Siebe Gorman and Company Ltd

Pneumatic face seal dust respirator

The pneumatic cushion in the *Type X* respirator moulds itself to the wearer's face. This ensures very little leakage (maximum 0.5%) when the wearer is speaking. It has a circular filter box which provides a large filtering area and offers less breathing resistance.

Inv. no. 1981–463
Presented by Martindale Protection Ltd

Gas and dust cartridge respirator

The *Model X* respirator, which covers nose and mouth only, filters out both gas and dust from polluted environments. The filters provide adequate protection against most gases at moderate concentrations. The mask has a replaceable cushion which moulds itself to the wearer's face.

Inv. no. 1981–464
Presented by Martindale Protection Ltd

Half mask respirator with spare filters

The AGA *Silner 12* is a two-filter respirator for protection against industrial dusts and gases. Different filters exist for a variety of gases and dusts and these can be used either separately or in pairs. The two-filter system gives the wearer a large surface area through which to breathe, thus reducing the 'breathing resistance'. Both

the canister and dust filters are easily and quickly installed.

Inv. no. 1981–1461, 1462
Presented by AGA Spiro Ltd

Welding respirator

The Safir *Twinair* has a half-face mask with an exhale valve built into the face piece. The dust cartridge is worn on the back, well away from welding fumes, and is connected to the mask, via two pipes worn over the shoulder. The welder's helmet can therefore be worn without any obstruction from the respirator.

Inv. no. 1982–156
Presented by Totectors Ltd

Full face mask respirator with sectioned filter and dust and ammonia filters

The AGA *Riva* face mask has a 40 mm thread connector which allows it to be used either with an airline or filter cartridges. The face-sealing edge minimises in-leakage and the large visor permits a wide field of view. Below the inner mask are demisting ports. These allow some of the filtered, inhaled air to flow inside the visor to eliminate condensation during long periods of use. Spectacles can be attached to rubber studs on the mask frame. As with the half-face mask (Inv. no. 1981–1461) a selection of filters is available.

The sectioned filter gives protection against all acid gases and vapours and also dust particles larger than 0.3 μm (3/10,000 mm).

Inv. no. 1981–1463, 1464
Presented by AGA Spiro Ltd

Protective respirator

This simple aluminium framed protective mask covering nose and mouth, can be used with a range of different filter pads for protection against industrial dust. First introduced in 1928 the mask has proved very successful; it was very popular during the thick London smogs of the early 1950s. The mask also prevents moisture or heat of exhaled breath contaminating precision instruments during assembly.

Inv. no. 1981–468　　Neg 1098/82/8
196/82 with Inv. nos.
1980–771, 1981–1521, 1982–421
Presented by Martindale Protection Ltd

Disposable paper respirator

This simple mask gives protection against nuisance dust particles.

Inv. no. 1982–155　　Neg 177/84
Presented by Totectors Ltd

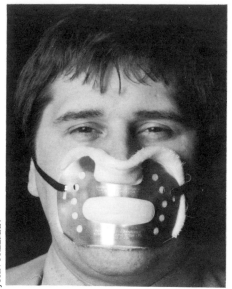

Aluminium framed, dust and vapour respirator, Inv no 1981–468

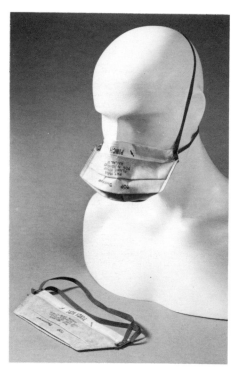

Disposable folded paper respirator, Inv no 1982–155

Disposable paper respirator

The *Aircare (5051)* mask folds flat when not in use and is designed to meet the requirements of BS 6016 type 2 filters. It is suitable for use in environments containing non-toxic dust.

Inv. no. 1983–1196
Presented by Racal Safety Ltd

Disposable particle dust respirator

The *Martindale* dust mask is pre-shaped and has a weight of only ⅛ oz. It is suitable for use in conditions where the

dust particle size is greater than 10 μm. There are two examples in the collection, one is sectioned.

Inv. no. 1981–466
Presented by Martindale Protection Ltd

Dust and fume respirator with exhale valve

This simple disposable mask filters out welding fumes. The exhale valve eases breathing and the steel clip holds the respirator against the bridge of the nose.

Inv. no. 1982–81   Neg 1099/82/5
Presented by 3M (United Kingdom) PLC

Disposable non-toxic particle respirator with nose grip

This simple dust mask has a steel nose clip which the wearer can 'pinch' over the bridge of the nose for a closer fit.

Inv. no. 1982–82
Presented by 3M (United Kingdom) PLC

Disposable dust respirators

These simple respirators, moulded from compressed fibres, provide the wearer with up to 90% protection against very fine dust. They are used in mining, laboratories and elsewhere. One respirator has been sectioned.

Inv. no. 1981–467
Presented by Martindale Protection Ltd

Disposable dust respirator

Intended for heavy industrial or agricultural use, this moulded fibre dust mask meets the requirements of BS 6016 type 2. The unusual shape, (there is an indentation in its convex surface), allows it to expand and contract as the wearer breathes while maintaining a good seal to the face.

Inv. no. 1983–1195   Neg 234/84
Presented by Racal Safety Ltd

Dust hood

A woven nylon fabric hood (type NA/6) is designed to provide short period protection from non-toxic dust. It has a 6 inch deep plastic visor and covers the head and the top of the shoulders. Under-arm straps are supplied to secure the hood. Breathing takes place through the weave of the material which acts as a simple respirator.

Inv. no. 1981–594
Presented by Safety Products Ltd

Nuisance odour respirator

This simple disposable mask in charcoal impregnated fibre covers the nose and mouth and protects against nuisance dust and odours.

Inv. no. 1982–420
Presented by Racal Safety Ltd

Nuisance odour respirator with exhale valve

This mask is similar to Inv. no. 1982–420 but is fitted with a plastic (non-return) valve for low breathing resistance.

Inv. no. 1982–421
                    Neg 196/82 with Inv. nos.
Presented by   1980–771, 1981–468,
Racal Safety Ltd   1981–1521

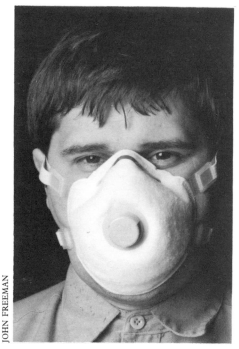

Disposable dust and fume respirator with exhale valve, Inv no 1982–81

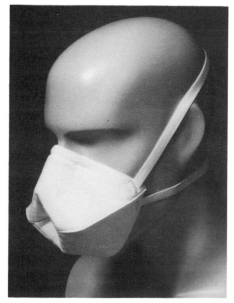

Disposable dust respirator, Inv no 1983–1195

Positive pressure

A breathing apparatus mask should fit the wearer's face and keep out all harmful air. However the human face comes in such a variety of shapes that it is impossible to manufacture a range of sizes to fit everyone.

Instead, the 'positive pressure' system is used, which raises air pressure inside the mask above that of the surrounding atmosphere. By this means any leakage around the mask is always from the wearer to the outside.

Figure 1 shows the 'breathing curve' for a system without positive pressure. Breathing in, pressure in the mask falls below that of the surrounding atmosphere and so polluted air could be drawn in.

Figure 2 shows the curve for a positive pressure system. Even when breathing in, air inside the mask is at higher pressure than outside, so there is no risk of inward leakage.

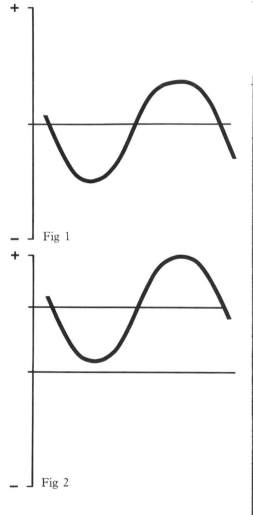

Fig 1

Fig 2

Filtered air ventilated helmet, the *Airstream* 1980, Inv no 1980–771

Positive pressure breathing mask

The rubber AGA *Spiromatic* full-face mask has a replaceable visor, provision for spectacles and space for a radio microphone.

'Dead space' in the mask is kept small by means of an inner mask covering the nose and mouth; this minimises the rebreathing of carbon dioxide enriched exhaled air. This inner mask has inhalation and exhalation ports which coincide with channels in the breathing valve ensuring that the inhaled and exhaled air never mix.

The demand valve is designed to give a slight positive pressure, around 200 Pa (200 N/m²), in the mask and the positive pressure is automatically activated when the user first inhales.

The mask is designed for use with breathing apparatus able to supply *at least* 300 litres/min at the mask connection.

Inv. no. 1983–600
Lent by AGA Spiro Ltd

Clean air helmet and visor

The *Airstream* helmet provides, by means of a fan and filtering system, clean dust-free air for the wearer. Dusty air is drawn into the rear of the helmet by a fan whose motor is driven by a battery carried on the belt. The filter pad is 95% efficient for dust particles of 0.5µm (5/10,000 mm), or greater, in size. Clean air then passes down the visor over the wearer's face. The forced air supply is such that there is always a positive pressure region near the wearer's mouth which prevents inhalation of any dusty air. The helmet also provides the wearer with head and eye protection and can be adapted for use by welders and people working close to radiant heat.

Inv. no. 1980–771   Neg 1097/82/12
Presented by   196/82 with Inv. nos.
Racal Safety Ltd   1981–468, 1981–1521,
1982–421

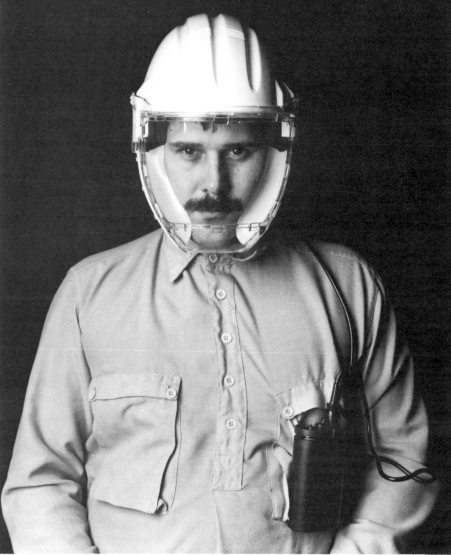

JOHN FREEMAN

Lightweight air-supplied visor

The lightweight, low cost *Dustmaster* gives respiratory protection in circumstances where head protection is not required, eg, veterinary and medical use. The visor is to BS 2092 grade 2 and the head cover and face seal are made from *Tyvek*. The belt-mounted air supply unit is battery powered and draws air through an easily replaceable filter. Three filter types are available: for non-toxic nuisance dusts, for fine dust not immediately hazardous to health and for non-toxic dust plus odour removal.

Inv. no. 1983–1194
Lent by Racal Safety Ltd

Clean air helmet

This helmet protects the wearer's head, eyes and lungs. The system of operation is similar to the *Airstream* helmet (Inv. no. 1980–771) except that the battery, fan and filter are built into the back of the helmet which covers the whole head and face.

Inv. no. 1981–460
Presented by Martindale Protection Ltd

Air supplied helmet

Fresh filtered air is supplied with an airline for breathing and for keeping the visor clear of condensation. The *White Knight* helmet is not tiring to wear, as its weight rests on the shoulders.

Inv. no. 1982–183
Presented by RFD Inflatables Ltd

Liquid air breathing apparatus *c.* 1906*

This is an example of the *Aerolith*, the first liquid-air breathing apparatus. Designed in 1901 by Otto Suess an Austrian mining engineer, it was brought to England in 1906 by the manufacturer's agent Otto Simonis.
Within the insulated leather covered box is a container holding nine pints of liquid air, sufficient for about 1½ hours' normal use. As the liquid evaporates air passes through a thin tube to the mouthpiece. Exhaled air passes through the main box, into the breathing bag, and out into the atmosphere. The *Aerolith* has no valves to separate inspired and expired air, so the latter is only carried away from the mouth by incoming fresh air. For this to be effective the liquid air must evaporate to create a flow of at least 30 litres per minute through the apparatus. In 1910 Col. W C Blackett added a purifying cartridge for absorbing carbon dioxide and moisture in the exhaled air, enabling it to be re-breathed.

Inv. no. 1981–2230, 1930–497 Neg 908/83
Lent by Durham and Northumberland Colliery, Fire and Rescue Brigade

Liquid oxygen breathing apparatus *c.* 1980

Modern liquid oxygen sets are generally similar to the early sets such as the *Aerolith* (Inv. no. 1981–2230). However liquid oxygen has superseded liquid air and the sets have become more efficient, compact and easier to maintain. The *Aerorlox* liquid oxygen set is designed for rescue and maintenance work in toxic atmospheres. It was first introduced in 1970.
Evaporated oxygen enters the breathing bag and mixes with purified exhaled air which has passed from the exhale tube through the soda lime canister and been cooled by passing over the end of the liquid oxygen container. As this moist purified air mixes with cold oxygen gas it loses about three-quarters of its moisture by condensation. On inhalation, the air enriched with fresh oxygen gas passes over the main portion of the evaporator where it is further dried and cooled; it then passes to the mask.
Since it produces cool, dry air, which is capable of removing body heat by evaporation, it is ideally suited for use in areas subject to high temperatures. It is widely used in mine rescue and fire fighting.

Inv. no. 1981–400   Neg 840/83
Lent by Siebe Gorman & Co Ltd

Liquid air breathing apparatus, the *Aerolith* c1906, Inv no 1981–2230, 1930–497

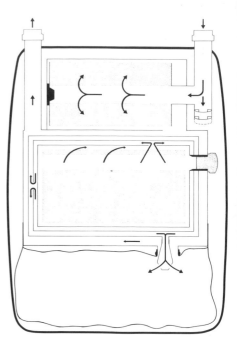

Operation of the *Aerorlox* breathing apparatus, inv. no. 1981–400

'Proto' breathing apparatus *c.* 1950*

The *Proto (Mk IV)* apparatus is a self-contained breathing set working on the regenerative principle whereby the same air is breathed continuously. Carbon dioxide in the exhaled air is absorbed by soda-lime contained in the breathing bag. The oxygen deficiency is then made up by air from the high pressure steel cylinder, which allows up to 2 hours continuous use under normal working conditions. The *Proto* is probably the best known of all breathing sets. The design is based upon the set patented by H A Fleuss in 1879. Sets were manufactured by Siebe Gorman & Co Ltd and many were used at the Seaham Colliery disaster of 1880. The design was considerably improved by R H Davis & L Hill in 1902. Since then the *Proto* has been widely used up to the present day, mainly for mine rescue and recovery and general work in poisonous atmospheres.

Inv. no. 1980–14   Neg 837/83, 1346/80
Purchased   1347/80

Compressed air breathing apparatus *c.* 1960

The AGA *Divator Universal 1* was designed for fire fighting, as well as diving. An anodised aluminium carrier plate reduces the weight of the apparatus, an important consideration if the set is worn for long periods. The breathing valve is designed so that 'breathing resistance' is as low as possible, enabling the wearer to breathe without undue effort. When the tank pressure reaches a critical level its reserve supply is activated manually by turning the reserve air valve.

Inv. no. 1983–599   Neg 836/83
Lent by AGA Spiro Ltd

Compressed air breathing apparatus, c. 1966

The *Airmaster* was introduced in the early 1960s by Siebe Gorman and Co Ltd. The single cylinder contains air at 135 atmospheres giving a duration of about 1 hour for moderately exacting work. It has a moulded rubber face mask with full-face clear-view visor, which incorporates the demand valve and exhalation valve. These valves work in a 'change-over' sequence that ensures the wearer receives only compressed air when breathing in. The action of breathing out closes the demand valve and operates the exhalation valve to the atmosphere.

Inv. no. 1983–272
Presented by the Eastern Electricity Board

Positive pressure, compressed air breathing apparatus c. 1980

The Chubb *No. 1 Mk 2* breathing set is a compressed air open-circuit type used for fire fighting and rescue operations and for prolonged work in toxic atmospheres. Mounted on either side of the face mask are a speech transmission diaphragm and a spring loaded exhale valve. This valve ensures that there is always a positive pressure region inside the mask to stop inward leakage of toxic fumes. The cylinder when charged to 200 bar, gives just under one hour's supply. A whistle warns the user when the air supply is running low.

Inv. no. 1983–1351   Neg 839/83
Lent by Chubb Panorama Ltd

Compressed air breathing set 1982

The *Firefighter* positive pressure breathing apparatus can supply up to about 56 minutes of fresh air to the user. It is designed to operate over a wide temperature range (−29°C to 70°C) and is fitted with a speech diaphragm, pressure warning whistle and an auxilliary air line attachment.

A feature of this particular set is that, in emergencies, it can function under water. For example at a dockside fire a fireman wearing this set could jump into the water to rescue someone who is trapped in a flooded hole or who has jumped overboard to escape.

Inv. no. 1983–1069   Neg 838/83
Lent by Siebe Gorman & Co Ltd

Breathing apparatus, the *Proto Mk. IV* c1950, Inv no 1980–14

Compressed air emergency escape apparatus

The *ELSA* is a compressed-air breathing set, having a maximum duration of six minutes. It allows the wearer to make a safe, quick escape in emergency situations, such as a large escape of toxic gas. It comprises a transparent plastic hood attached by an airline to a small gas bottle carried in a simple tabard.

Inv. no. 1980–1046
Lent by Sabre Safety Ltd

Emergency escape respirator and hood

The Draeger *Parat* mask was designed for use in emergency situations where there is a high concentration of smoke and fumes. The mask would be kept in a box in an accessible position. To prevent deterioration the respirator is kept in a sealed aluminium foil bag containing silica gel to absorb any moisture. The filter offers protection against all known fumes that occur after fires, and the hood is of flame-retardant material that can withstand temperatures in excess of 1,000°C for several seconds. Two specimens are preserved, one has been taken from its foil bag.

Inv. no. 1981–1486
Presented by Draeger Safety Ltd

Emergency escape smoke mask

The *Breathing Space* smoke mask completely covers the head of the wearer. It is made from flame retardant material and has a flame retardant transparent PVC visor. Protection against smoke and fumes is provided by a built-in filter pad. It is held on to the head by a chinstrap. It can be stored in a wall-hung dispenser and one size of mask fits adults and children.

Inv. no. 1982–56
Presented by Peter Black (Keighley) Ltd

Sportswear

Apart from the risk of fire in motor racing all sporting protective wear is concerned with reducing the effect of impacts on the body. Many sports which in their origin date back to ancient times have always had certain pieces of equipment designed to protect. These were often rudimentary and gave only the minimum safeguards; public opinion requires that in modern sports the risk of accidental injury is reduced to the minimum possible bearing in mind the particular nature of a sport. Modern plastics have provided opportunities to considerably improve the equipment available. Padding materials at one time were confined to such things as horsehair, rags and straw; now a range of lightweight foamed plastics with high resistance to crushing and a good level of resilience can be used.

Replica protective skull cap as used by cricketer Mike Brearley in 1976, Inv no 1982–664

Cricketer's protective equipment 1981

The game of cricket has been played in England for over 650 years and it has evolved to the extent that, in some instances, a player's personal safety can be at risk. The modern batsman can protect himself with a large range of protective clothing. The exhibits comprise a helmet, pads for the legs, a thigh pad, a 'box', batting gloves and batting boots. The helmet has a removable visor and alternative temple-guards.

Inv. no. Helmet 1981–1323,
Boots 1981–410, Leg and Thigh Pads,
Batting Gloves and Box 1980–835

Helmet presented by Duncan Fearnley
Boots presented by W Little & Sons Ltd
Pads, gloves and box lent by Stuart
Surridge Ltd

Cricket helmet 1976 (replica)

After facing the West Indian fast bowling in 1976 Mike Brearley and Tony Greig of the England Team decided that they needed protective head gear. A surgical appliance firm made the originals, using the technique by which they made helmets for epileptic children. Each man's helmet was cast on a wax mould of his own head, with ventilation holes so that it fitted comfortably under his cap. The material of the helmet was polyethylene, approximately 3mm (1/8 in.) thick.

Inv. no. 1982–664   Neg 257/84
Purchased

Football boots 1980

Footballers originally played in their everyday shoes. However around 1860, some players took to wearing navvy's boots which had heavy metal toe caps. The navvy's boot continued to influence the style of football boots until after the 1939–45 War.

The modern lightweight-style boots were first worn on the Continent and were introduced into England during the early 1950s. The specimens in the collection were worn by the West Ham and England player Trevor Brooking MBE, during the 1980–81 season.

Inv. no. 1981–2127
Presented by Trevor Brooking MBE

Goalkeeping gloves for wet and dry conditions 1980

The first pair of gloves are worn in dry conditions with the synthetic grip spots on the palm; in wet conditions they are reversed and the knitted nylon side is worn on the palm. The second pair are designed to be worn in all weather conditions.

Inv. nos. 1983–1063, 1983–1062
Lent by Bryan-Grasshopper Ltd

Fencing jacket *c.* 1932

The jacket is in heavy-duty canvas padded with horsehair.

Inv. no. 1981–699
Presented by Sir David Follett

Motorcycle racing leathers 1980

The first two-piece leather motor-cycling suits were introduced in the early 1920s; the trousers developed from riding breeches. Coloured leathers were introduced in 1960, until that date they were either black or dark brown. The leathers in the collection were worn by Mick Grant, winner of the Formula 1 Class in the Isle of Man TT Race in 1980. They were designed by Interstate Leathers for the *Honda* Works Team. The one-piece suit is made from racing quality (1.2mm) leather and is lined with *Aertex*, a perforated nylon material, which enables the leather to 'breathe' in hot weather. For extra ventilation air vents are situated under the arms. Vulnerable areas on the shoulders, tops of the arms, elbows, hips, knees and the seat have a double layer of leather. The one-piece suit was first introduced in 1950 by the rider Geoff Duke.

Inv. no. 1981–597
Presented by Interstate Leathers

Waxed cotton motorcyle suit 1981
Black waxed cotton, quilted nylon lining

Made from waterproof waxed cotton, the *Trialmaster Trophy* suit is lined with quilted nylon to retain body heat. Vents at the shoulders and under the arms reduce perspiration. Extra reinforcing is provided at the shoulders, elbows, hips and inside legs.

The suit is also fitted with a reversible retro-reflective belt and safety triangle. This helps to reduce accidents, by making the motor cyclist more conspicuous. The suit can retain its normal appearance by reversing the belt and folding away the safety triangle.

Inv. no. 1981–407
Presented by Belstaff International Ltd

Lightweight motorcycle suit 1981
Polyurethane coated nylon

This *Bergen* suit is a one-piece design intended to give freedom of movement and all weather protection. Its bright colour makes it more conspicuous when the visibility is poor. The zip is covered by a layer of material and the seat and crutch of the trousers are reinforced. This particular example is intended for a lady.

Inv. no. 1981–580
Presented by Rivetts of London Ltd

Motorcyclist's boots 1983

These *Grand Prix* boots are intended for riders taking part in competition work and racing. The boots have internal steel toe caps and heat and oil resistant soles in nitrile rubber, and there is added protection for the shins.

Inv. no. 1983–834
Presented by George Ward Footwear Ltd

Foamed plastic body protection pads

These pads represent a type of protection intended for use by motorcyclists, bobsledders and the like. Made from a foamed plastic, *Plastozote*, the pads would be worn under the outer clothing and comprise the following:
back and front chest pads – linked together
two sets of forearm, elbow, and upper arm pads – linked together
two sets of thigh, knee and calf pads – linked together
a pair of shoulder pads
a pair of hip pads
genital protector (box)

Inv. no. 1984–187
Presented by A V Armorpli Ltd

Motor racing driver's outfit 1980
Nomex III coveralls, balaclava and boots, fibreglass helmet with 1mm Lexan visor

The driver's major hazard is fire, a risk that increased with the switch from alcohol to petrol fuels in 1958.

The coverall and helmet of this outfit belonged to Alan Jones, the 1980 Formula 1 World Champion. The outer coverall has 3 layers of *Nomex III* with interleaving of *Kynol*; this combination affords about 50 seconds protection in a petrol fire. Strong epaulettes are sewn onto the shoulders enabling the driver to be pulled out of the car in an emergency. The helmet is one of those tailor-made for Alan Jones and is based on a design of the standard *X80* motor racing helmet. It is made from fire resistant fibreglass with an unbreakable, fire resistant 1mm *Lexan* visor. The field of view is much smaller than motor cycle racing helmets because of the greater dangers of flying debris. Inside the helmet is a 28mm layer of impact-absorbing foam. The helmet also has an air injection point for the emergency air system which will force about 30 seconds of compressed air into the driver's helmet when activated by a push-button and save the driver from inhaling toxic fumes during his escape from the car should there be a fire.

Inv. no. 1982–175 coverall, 1982–145 helmet, 1982–772 boots, 1982–149 gloves, 1983–1353 balaclava
Coverall presented by Alan Jones, helmet lent by Euro-Helmets Ltd, balaclava presented by Road and Racing Accessories Ltd, boots presented by Edward Lewis Shoes Ltd, gloves presented by Bury & Hopwood Ltd

Neg 232/84

Rally driver's coverall 1982
Zirpro-treated wool

The one-piece coverall garment is typical of that worn by racing and rally drivers and meets the current Federal Automotive Institute test for flame-resistant clothing to be worn by racing drivers. For this test, the subject's forearm, protected by the coverall and underwear of the same material, must survive exposure by burning fuel for at least 20 seconds.

In an emergency, rescuers can pull the driver clear of the car by strengthened epaulettes attached to the coverall.

Inv. no. 1983–1060
Lent by the International Wool Secretariat

Alan Jones's Formula 1 racing outfit 1980,
Inv. no. 1982–175

Fitted to the helmet is a wire face mask, made from epoxy coated steel and a high density polycarbonate throat protector. The shoulder and arm pads are made from nylon covered foam and are designed to give a high degree of mobility and protection. They are tapered to fit neatly into the goal mitts. The body pad is made from *Rubatex* foam covered and lined with waterproof nylon. Knee pads are worn under the goal pads and are made from foam covered in *Nylite* and vinyl. The goal pads are stuffed with foam padding and covered in good quality cowhide. The side gussets are made from *Nylite* and the backing is white felt. The stick hand mitt has a sheet of polyethylene sandwiched between polyfoam and leather. The thumb protector is padded with foam and reinforced with polyethylene. The catching mitt is made from double ply two-piece leather and the palm has polyethylene stiffeners sandwiched between the felt. The goalkeeper also wears a genital protector (not in collection). The elaborate outfit is intended to give full protection against all the impact hazards the wearer may meet.

Inv. no. 1983–1073
Lent by W H Fagan & Son Ltd, courtesy Cooper Canada Ltd

Boxer's sparring equipment 1982

This comprises sparring gloves, specially designed headguard and an abdominal protector.

When in the ring the professional fighter is currently allowed to wear only the abdominal protector and gloves, which must not weigh more than 6 oz for flyweight to light middleweight and 8 oz for middleweight to heavyweight bouts. The hands, but not the knuckles, can be bandaged; up to 8ft of soft bandage on each hand. All fighters also wear gum shields to protect the teeth and gums.

Inv. no. 1983–1064   Neg 841/83
Lent by Bryan-Grasshopper Ltd

Ice hockey goalkeeper's outfit 1982

The outfit comprises helmet and mask, throat protector, a pair of shoulder and arm pads, body pad, pants, pair of knee pads, pair of goal pads, catch mitt, stick hand mitt, braces, garter belt, pair of socks, pair of ice skates, sweater (sectioned) and goalstick.

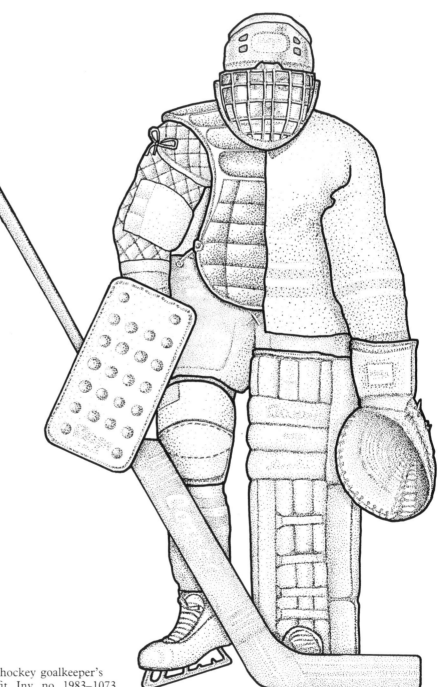

Ice hockey goalkeeper's
outfit, Inv. no. 1983–1073

60

Ice hockey outfield player's protective girdle 1982

This new type of girdle protection was introduced by Cooper Canada in the early 1980s and protects the thighs, tail bone, hips, kidneys and abdomen. It is constructed from a double layer of *Lycra*. The padding, which does not absorb moisture, is moulded to conform to the shape of the body. The inner surface is also nubbed to allow ventilation.

Inv. no. 1983–1075
Lent by W H Fagan & Son Ltd, courtesy Cooper Canada Ltd

Plastic face mask for ice hockey

The moulded face mask was devised by Jacques Plante in 1963–64. Nowadays a wire mask is preferred since close fitting moulded masks of this type tend to pass part of any impact onto the face.

Inv. no. 1983–1074
Lent by W H Fagan & Son Ltd, courtesy Cooper Canada Ltd

Rugby League protective equipment

Many Rugby League players, especially forwards, wear shoulder, knee and head protection. Shoulder pads can reduce injury such as fractures of the humerus and collar bone or dislocation of the shoulder. Knee pads are especially useful when the ground is hard. Many players also wear gumshields to protect their teeth and gums. The examples in the collection are shoulder pads in white polyvinyl chloride (PVC) with sponge inserts. The knee pads are made in *Plastazote* (low density polyethylene foam) and the gum shield is in high density plastic. A new style of shoulder pad was introduced into the UK from Australia in the mid 1970s. The *Perseus* shoulder pads in the collection are of this new type. They are light-weight (under 600 grams) and are padded with 98% waterproof impact-absorbing inserts. The pads extend over the shoulder to help reduce injuries when tackling opposing players.

Inv. no. 1981–2173 knee and shoulder pads, 1982–555 gumshield,
Pads presented by Medisport Developments, gumshield presented by Newitt & Co Ltd

Stages of preparation of a gumshield

The specimens comprise a mouth guard impression kit and instruction sheet, a mouth guard impression, a model cast from the mouth guard impression and a completed mouth guard.

Inv. no. 1982–518
Presented by Sportsafety Ltd

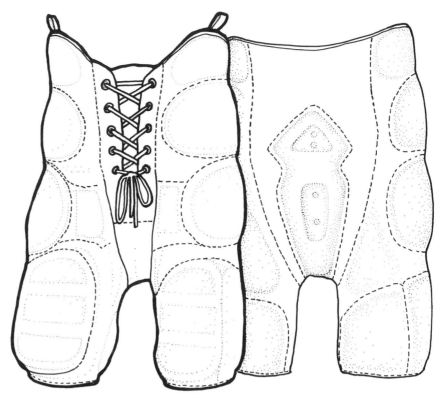

Ice hockey outfield player's protective girdle, inv. no. 1983–1075

Men's running shoes 1950

Spiked running shoes were first introduced in the 1850s. Modern shoes have interchangeable spikes. These shoes were used by Sir David Follett, a former Director of the Museum, during the 1950s.

Inv. no. 1981–700
Presented by Sir David Follett

American football helmet 1982 (sectioned)

The earliest American football helmets were based on the leather flying helmets which appeared around 1910. This type has long been superseded by the plastic helmet, first introduced in 1939. The sectioned example in the collection has a reinforced plastic shell lined with *Ensolite*, a closed cell foam which has excellent shock absorbing properties. There are also inflatable bladders attached to the inside of the helmet which can be pumped up like a bicycle tyre for extra protection.

Inv. no. 1982–775
Presented by Uniroyal Ltd   Neg 176/84

American football shoulder pads and helmet (child size), 1980

The *Century* shoulder pads have three separate, but overlapping, plastic plates on either shoulder. This design allows flexibility and freedom of arm movement. Upper rib protection is provided by plastic guards; the right and left sections of the pads are connected together by laces.

The high density plastic helmet has removable foam inserts (*Isosorb*) which protect the ears, back, crown and front of the head. The face guard is plastic-coated metal.

In addition to these two items the footballer would wear thigh and leg protection under the uniform.

Inv. no. 1983–1065
Purchased

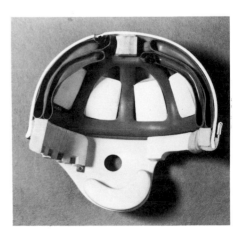

American footballer's helmet 1982, (sectioned), Inv. no. 1982–775

Fishing wader and boots

This breast-high sock wader has adjustable elastic braces and is made in polyurethane-coated nylon with an inflatable air chamber at chest level which increases the bouyancy giving protection should the wearer slip and fall in fast running water. The *Gamesman*, blucher style, lacing ankle boots are intended to be worn with the breast-high wader and come just above the ankle with styrene rubber soles and heels studded to give extra grip on slippery rocks.

Inv. no. 1981–665, 1981–666
Lent by Uniroyal Ltd

Climber's weatherproof suit 1981
Gore-tex fabric

The lightweight material of this *Annapurna* outfit protects the climber against driving rain as the hood, wrists and waist are elasticated and the zipper is covered by an overflap which is held down by *Velcro*. *Gore-tex* fabric has been used to make the suit as it will allow water vapour from the climber's body to escape while maintaining the proof of the material against heavy rain.

Inv. no. 1981–405
Presented by Belstaff International Ltd

Climber's jacket 1981

The *Peak* thermal pile jacket replaces the need for many layers of ordinary clothing.
The pile traps a warm layer of insulating air close to the body. Since the pile is soft it can be worn next to the skin. The jacket gives excellent all-weather protection if worn in conjunction with a waterproof oversuit like Inv. no. 1981–405.

Inv. no. 1981–406
Presented by Belstaff International Ltd

Alpine jacket and plus twos overtrousers, 1924 (replicas)

The Alpine or Himalayan climber of the 1920s wore ordinary clothes for protection against the cold.
A typical outfit comprised a Harris tweed Norfolk Jacket and plus twos overtrousers. Under these were worn woollen underwear, a flannel shirt and several sweaters. Footwear consisted of several pairs of thick socks, puttees, and leather boots. These examples are replicas of those used on the 1924 Everest expedition.

Inv. no. 1981–794
Presented by Burberrys Ltd

Everest expedition outfit, 1933

Items worn by Sir Jack Longland during the unsuccessful attempt on Mount Everest in 1933 comprise:
1 Pair of silk inner gloves.
2 Pair of overmitts.
3 Windproof overall suit. This is made from Grenfell cloth (a new development at that time), which allowed body moisture to pass through but stopped water penetrating to the wearer.
4 Two Shetland wool lightweight sweaters.
5 Pair of lightweight double clinker-nailed climbing boots (by R. Lawries and Co.)
6 Tibetan fur cap as used by Sherpas and Muleteers
7 Pair of sheepskin boots (by Morland and Co.)

Inv. no. 1981–812
Presented by Sir Jack Longland

Silk long johns, 1976

Worn during the successful British/ Nepalese expedition to the summit of Everest in 1976. Climbers have found (as Chris Bonington points out in 'Everest the Hard Way') that silk provides not only insulation against the cold but also protection against the hot sun.

Inv. no. 1981–796
Presented by Major M W H Day

Indian puttees, 1922

These puttees, each of which is over 10 ft (3.2m) long, were worn by Dr T G Longstaff during the 1922 Everest expedition (*Puttee* is derived from the Hindu word *patti* meaning band or bandage.)

Inv. no. 1981–797
Presented by Mrs C Longstaff

Fibre pile mountaineering jacket, 1978

Identical to those used on the successful 1978 'without oxygen' Everest expedition. The garment proved so popular on that climb that many expeditions requested similar jackets for their climbs.
It has two large 'camera' pockets and an integral hood with a split mouth shield which can be fastened by *Velcro*.
The outer material is non-pilling (i.e. it does not fluff or ball-up so retaining its appearance and fibre insulating qualities.)

Inv. no. 1981–803
Presented by Southern Safety Equipment

Jockey's protective equipment 1981

The helmet (1) is made from glass fibre with the surface sanded and coated with white paint to stop the jockey's hat slipping off during a race. High impact plastic lens goggles (2) keep mud and dust out of the jockey's eyes. The back protector (3) in *Plastazote* a low density polyethylene foam pad is shaped to fit the jockey's back. Back protectors have been worn intermittently for some 10 years. If a jockey wears contact lenses (and only the 'soft' type are allowed) he or she must wear a contact lens tag (4). If an accident occurs a doctor can then remove the contact lenses before any damage is done.

Inv. no. 1: 1981–855 2: 1982–29 3:1982–28 4:1981–1550
1: Presented by Champion Horse and Clothing Manufacturers Ltd
4: Presented by The Jockey Club

Sport diver's wet suit 1981

Following developments in underwater breathing apparatus made during the Second World War the new sport of skindiving appeared. In cold water areas the body loses heat very quickly and this kind of suit appeared in the 1950s as a method of combating this loss. It comprises a jacket, 'long johns', socks and hood in 6mm neoprene material. The neoprene is in the form of a microcellular foam which, fitting close to the body, traps a layer of water close to the skin. This layer of water warms up to some extent and provides a layer of insulation additional to that provided by the air bubbles in the foam itself. However, as the foam is compressible its insulating effect is reduced as the diver goes deeper. Also preserved with the suit are a schnorkel tube, mask and fins.

Inv no. 1981–408
Presented by Typhoon International Ltd

Test apparatus and test specimens

The development of test apparatus specifically for protective wear mainly dates from the 1950s although equipment for carrying out evaluations of fabrics' performance aided textile scientists for many years before then. The establishment of British Standards covering certain articles of safety wear led to the construction of closely-specified test apparatus. The impact and penetration testing of vehicle users' helmets is an example of this; the flammability test for textiles another. The museum's collection includes only a few items in this field but it is hoped to acquire more in the future.

Metal splash testing rig, 1977

In the past metal splash tests involved pouring a ladle of molten metal onto fabric held at various angles. Fabrics that did not burst into flames or disintegrate were considered suitable clothing materials.

In March 1977 the International Wool Secretariat, co-operating with the Health & Safety Executive, British Steel Corporation and other foundries, developed this test rig to simulate working conditions.

A measured volume of metal pours from the ladle onto refractory brick to create a controlled splash onto the fabric. Behind the fabric is a sheet of PVC film which, over a 5 second period, reacts like human skin; glazing or fracturing of this film being equivalent to second and third degree burns.

Inv. no. 1983–1061
Lent by The International Wool Secretariat.

Metal splash test samples

Four samples showing typical results when 50 grammes of molten aluminium at 800°C were poured onto them from about 15 centimetres, using a test rig.

1 *Asbestos* widely used as a shield against radiant heat. The metal has partly adhered and although it does not burn through heat is conducted to the back of the material damaging the simulated skin.
2 *Flame retardant cotton* a fabric which has been chemically treated to make it less inflammable. It has charred through leaving the skin burnt and partly adhering to the cloth.
3 *Aramid* a synthetic fabric which gives excellent protection against fire but here the aluminium has stuck to the surface, transmitting great heat through the cloth, destroying the skin.

4 *Zirpro treated wool* the fabric has been treated with a zirconium salt. The metal has only slightly scorched the surface as it rolled off and there is no damage to the skin.

Presented by the International Wool Secretariat   Neg 200/82
Inv. no. 1984–143

Safety footwear impact tester

The apparatus is used to test safety footwear toecaps. The weighted platform and striker, travelling on vertical guide rails, drops onto the toecap of the boot. The magnitude of the impact can be varied, according to the specified test, by changing the weights and the release height. A rebound device prevents a second impact occurring. A small plug of plasticine inside the toecap enables the distortion caused by the impact to be measured.

On this machine footwear can be tested to British Standard 953, German DIN 4843 and Belgian, Canadian, Italian, South African and United States of America standards.

Inv. no. 1983–1083
Lent by the Shoe and Allied Trade Research Association

The collection includes the following samples of materials, mostly small in size. The samples are held for reference purposes and are cross-indexed to the relevant inventory item.

Aluminised asbestos
Aluminised rayon
Asgard – five types
Ceramic terylene
Dacron – two types
Dartex
Deflam
Dunlopillo foam
Ensolite
Evazote
Firotex – two types
Flectalon
Fortamid – five types
Fyretex
Gore-tex membrane
Gore-tex – nine types
Grenfell cloth
Heatshield cloth
Jobflam
Karvin
Keylar
Nylon
Panotex – nine types
Plastazote
Polyester/vincel
Proban cotton – three types
Reflexite
Teklan 'Tufkem'
Terylene/cotton
Thinsulate – five types
Tyvek – fourteen types
Viscose rayon, acrylic bonded – six types

Book list

Few books deal directly with the development of specialised and protective wear. Many of the books on occupational costume are overly concerned with the more picturesque clothing worn at work and almost none with present-day wear. I give a short list of books which I have found of value, there are other references, short articles and pamphlets covering in part some aspects of this catalogue's subject but space does not allow a listing here.

Occupational Costume in England Cunnington and Lucas. A & C Black 1976 – this book has a chapter on protective clothing apart from many useful references in the remaining text.

Occupational Costume and Working Clothes 1796–1876 A Lansdell, Shire Publications 1977, 2nd edition 1984

Dressed for the Job C Williams-Mitchell, Blandford 1982

English Costume for Sport and Outdoor Recreation Cunnington and Mansfield, A & C Black 1964

Materials and Clothing in Health and Disease E T Renbourn, H K Lewis 1972

Deep Sea Diving and Submarine Operations R H Davis, reprinted Siebe Gorman 1982 – Besides its account of the history of diving dress the book contains useful information on breathing apparatus.

Flying Clothing Harold and Greer, Airlife 1979

The Dangerous Sky D H Robinson, G T Foulis 1973 – a history of aviation medicine but the book covers many aspects of specialised flying wear like oxygen apparatus, heated clothing etc.

Suiting Up For Space L. I. Mallen, John Day (New York) 1971

Available from the Science Museum shop, *Covering Up* by John Smart and John Griffiths published by the Science Museum 1982, price 80 pence.

Donor and lender index

Index

to catalogue entries